Operation Scorched Arse

R Humphries

Woodettes Publications

Published 2009
by
Woodettes Publications
Houston, Texas, USA

© Woodettes Publications 2009

R Humphries has asserted his right to be identified as the author of this work with all rights reserved including the right of reproduction in whole or in part in any form.

The Library of Congress has catalogued this edition as follows Humphries, R [date]
Operation Scorched Arse : a novel by R Humphries
1st Ed.

ISBN 978-0-578-02671-8

www.woodettes.wordpress.com

Author's Note

This is a work of fiction. Names, characters, places and incidents are either the product of the author's imagination or are used fictitiously. Any resemblance to actual events or locales or persons, living or dead, is entirely coincidental.

The stories based at the Woody Back to School Unit are works of adult fiction based upon the real-life fantasy games played by the author, R. Humphries and his wife, the inimitable Jojo.

It is the author's intent to create the Woody Back to School Unit as an imaginative world peopled with a believable cast and set in familiar surroundings within which the readers will become comfortable.

The vernacular used in the stories is a combination of the phraseology derived from writing such as the British penny comics from the nineteen thirties, current language, slang and idioms, and the invented parlance known as Woody Jargon.

As such references to 'beating', 'thrashing', and 'flogging' have no context to the use or avocation of physical violence, with the exception of controlled corporal punishment, against the characters of the stories.

**Dedicated
to
My Beloved Jojo**

Contents

Public Enemy Number One 1
Guidelines for Extreme Scolding 5
Running Benders 9
A Sound Beating 13
Anatomy of a Running Bender 17
A Lunchtime Licking 21
A Low-Rider 25
Surprise, Surprise! 29
Nailing the Big BUTT 33
The Fabulous Fart 37
A Bare Bum Spanking 41
Bacon Slicers 45
The New SS 49
Caning Prefects 53
Scorched Arses 57
Anarchy and Chaos 61
A Disagreeable Start to the Day 65
A Ration of Tongue Pie 69
Extreme Prejudice 73
Extreme Malice 77
Miss Cathryn Cassidy 81
An Epic Scolding 85
A Poor Beleaguered Bum 89
The Woody Mantra 93
Jojo 97
The Fine Art of Dangling 101
Ivan Takes a Tumble 105
I'll Be Watching You 109
Sacrificial Bumbags 113
Cool Arse Christmas 117
Hot Arse Christmas 121
The Spice of Spanking 125

Public Enemy Number One

Jojo Heyworth's prediction that the inmates of the Woody Back to School unit were going to suffer a long, hot winter was proving unerringly accurate.

Just thirty-six hours after being publicly flogged for causing considerable damage by sneaking a horse into the chemistry laboratory Deborah Morton found herself up to her bumbags in another disagreeable situation.

The inmates were collecting their books ready for the start of the day's educational curriculum when the intercom crackled.

"Morton, Phase 5, repair immediately to the library to respond to charges of bringing the Red House into disrepute," barked the unmistakable voice of Katie Beck, the unit's Matron.

The inmates exchanged curious glances.

"What the dickens?" gasped Deborah.

"This does not sound good," was Jojo's learned opinion.

Operation Scorched Arse

Deborah gaped at the six prefects incredulously. "You have to be kidding me," she spluttered.

Patsy Butcher looked uncomfortable. "I'm sorry, Morton," she said. "The application has been filed under new protocols. The council has to consider it."

Patty Hodge, Katie Beck and the Wart were in their usual position propping up the bar in the Bunch of Grapes.

Patty Hodge and her cronies were discussing the 'Eyes Only' memorandum that Ms Lawton, the units Principal, had issued to the Brass and the Elite at the emergency summit to announce the new zero-tolerance campaign, code-named Operation Scorched Arse.

The content of the memorandum had assigned Deborah Morton the rank of the facility's new Public Enemy Number One and instructed the recipients to target her with 'Extreme Prejudice and the Utmost Hostility'.

"Oh man, we can sure have fun with this," cackled the Wart.

Katie grinned. "I've had this idea floating around for a while," she said conspiratorially. "This may be the perfect time to put it into action."

"Come on, Katie; spill the beans," grinned Patty, "what has that evil, bitchy mind of yours come up with this time?"

Patsy continued to look uncomfortable. "We've received official notification that you have been declared Public Enemy Number One," she told Debs.

"Some members of the House Council believe that under the new provisions of the House Charter that makes you guilty of bringing the Red House into disrepute."

Debs glared at the prefects. "What provisions?" she demanded.

"They are being ratified by the Mistress of the House as we speak," said Janet Mitchell smugly.

Cathryn Cassidy looked daggers at Mitch the Bitch. "They are not ratified yet you stupid bitch," she snarled.

"Oh but they will be," interjected Yvonne Godfrey, "you mark my words."

Deborah knew when she was being stitched up like a kipper. The prefectorial council presiding over the Red House was comprised of two of her chums, Patsy and Cat, and her four sworn enemies, Yvonne, Bitchypoo, Spanker Spage and Ivan the Terrible. Ms Wharton, the most despised member of the unit's Brass served as Mistress of the Red House and would ratify anything that could make life disagreeable for the inmates.

At first Patsy and Cathryn refused to hear the application and argued furiously with Yvonne and her cronies. At one point Patsy had to restrain Cat who looked ready to scratch Janet's eyes out. Finally a grubby arrived in the library and handed Patsy a document. Patsy read it quickly and then handed it to Cathryn.

"This is so bogus," Cat growled.

"I'm sorry Debs," groaned Patsy, "but we're going to have to take a vote."

Operation Scorched Arse

Deborah's arms and neck ached from facing the wall with her hands on her head and her nose pressed forward against the wood-paneling.

The council had voted and predictably she was found guilty by four votes to two.

"Ms Wharton is currently indisposed and cannot be disturbed," cackled Janet Mitchell, "we'll place you in House Custody until she is available."

"You cannot be serious," spluttered Debs.

"I am absolutely serious," the Wart assured her. "The protocols now require that you are subjected to a Full Collar Walkthrough and a Formal House Beating."

Deborah gaped at the Wart.

Guidelines for Extreme Scolding

"I'll try to make this as easy as possible," whispered Cat. "Try not to struggle and keep in step."

Deborah nodded miserably.

"Button down the landings," barked Katie Beck. "Mandatory six of the best for anybody caught goofing, gabbing, larking or pranking. Commence the escort."

Deborah Morton's cheeks turned a deep crimson as she entered the Elite landing. The six members of the Blue House were positioned outside the doors to their studies. The six members of the Red House were already congregated in the gymnasium ready to witness Deborah receiving the first ever Formal House Beating.

Cathryn had Deborah's right arm pulled up behind her back. The fingers of her left hand were inserted inside the collar of Deb's blouse. As gently as possible, Cat propelled Deborah along each of the seven landings. It was a laborious expedition.

Operation Scorched Arse

The landings were housed on four floors of the main building, the Elite had the whole top storey and the studies and dormitories of the lower phase inmates were spread out over the floors below.

Cat and Debs walked slowly so that Debs could keep pace. When they reached the stairwells between floors Cat released her grip on Debs so that she would be less likely to trip on the stairs.

Deborah's cheeks burned with humiliation. She couldn't recall feeling so mortified since she was publicly hand-cuffed on the center court of Wimbledon and carted off by the Dark Agents of the System.

The members of the Red House had formed a circle of bodies in the gymnasium. Deborah Morton and Patsy Butcher stood in the center. Debs was required to stand with her hands on her head while Patsy delivered the Official House Scolding.

It had been a tiresome and frustrating morning for Deborah. After learning of her fate she had been returned to the library and forced to resume her pose of nose and toes while the scolding was drafted.

Patsy had tried valiantly to make the scolding as brief and innocuous as possible. However, her preliminary drafts were rejected by the Wart who insisted that she beef the wording up in keeping with Ms Lawton's *'Guidelines for Extreme Scolding'*. For the duration Debs was forced to remain facing the wall with Yvonne Godfrey monitoring her intensely to ensure that her nose was permanently touching the panels and that at no time did her elbows inadvertently make contact with the wall.

The Official Public Scolding ran for almost five long minutes. All the while Debs was required to remain hands on head, eyes front and not move a muscle. Artfully Yvonne and Janet had positioned themselves directly in her line of vision and throughout the ignominious reprimand Deborah was constantly confronted by the prefects' coprophagic smirks.

Finally Deborah was allowed to lower her arms. Even though she had tried to block out much of the scripted scolding her face was still flushed with righteous indignation. The text that the Wart and Ms Lawton had finally approved had painted an appalling picture of degeneracy and depravity and completely ignored the significant contributions she had made to the Red House in terms of her scholastic, sporting and musical achievements. During her sentence at the unit Deborah had earned more merit marks for her House than any inmate in history. Nonetheless she knew that any attempt to defend her self would be pointless and besides she had rather more pressing matters on her mind.

Patsy Butcher took a deep breath. She was flexing the ceremonial house cane between her hands. Momentarily she handed the cane to Cathryn while she shrugged off her blazer. In blouse and skirt her superb athletic physique was even more apparent. The House Captain reached up and unfastened the collar of her blouse and then rolled up her sleeves before retrieving the cane. For an instant she caught Deborah's eye and they exchanged a glance of mutual resignation.

"Morton, you have been found guilty of bringing the Red House into disrepute and will receive a twelve-stroke running bender as punishment," Patsy said softly "Now please repair to the beam and prepare yourself to be beaten."

There was a hush in the gymnasium as the inmates separated to make way for Debs as she turned to walk towards the training beam that had been lowered from the ceiling track. With the exception of Yvonne, Janet and their sycophantic cronies the inmates lowered their heads in sympathy to Deborah's terrible plight.

Deborah did her best to keep her head up high but she averted her eyes and her naturally athletic gait seemed slightly inelegant as she trudged down the gymnasium. She reached the beam and slowly unfastened the top button of her red and black striped blazer. She shrugged the jacket off and folded it neatly across the beam. Deborah stretched out her arms and placed her hands on the beam. Very slowly she leaned forward.

Running Benders

Running Benders were nothing new. They had been invented by an athletic prefect named Gemima Appleby who wished to teach Claire Brooks a lesson for rubbishing her.

When Ms Lawton got wind of the novel technique she had been intrigued and had set up a test range in the gymnasium for Big Gem to give her a demonstration. The Grand Dame had been immediately impressed by Gemima's display of athleticism and dexterous control of the cane. However, she had some reservations and selected several prefects to participate in the running bender trials. As she suspected the technique was difficult to coordinate and even after several practice sessions few of the prefects could guarantee a clean caning.

Although Ms Lawton was of the opinion that gals were broad of beam and perfectly designed for being caned on the bottom she knew that the cane needed to land crisply on the crown of the rump. She had learned from her own experiences at school that

Operation Scorched Arse

a badly delivered caning could cause unnecessary discomfort.

Following the trials she issued a dictate that only prefects who could consistently prove themselves on the test range would be certified to deliver running benders.

Noticeably it was mostly the more athletic inmates who managed to perfect the tricky technique and Patsy Butcher was a world class athlete.

Deborah Morton and Patsy Butcher were close chums. Patsy often spotted Debs while she worked on her quick sprints. Nonetheless as Deborah approached the beam at the end of the hall she was in no doubt that the next few minutes would prove to be extremely unpleasant.

Despite their friendship, several days earlier, Patsy had been required to cane Deborah in another matter with regard to Red House Business. The caning had been a conventional close-in six of the best administered with the same ceremonial house cane. Deborah who had been caned by dozens of prefects during her career was of the opinion that Patsy ranked amongst the most proficient ever. The prospect of a twelve-stroke running bender from the athletic Rastafarian made Debs extremely nervous.

Ms Lawton had been impressed during the running bender trials. The Butcher twins were the first prefects ever to get full certification at their first attempt, each shooting perfect sixes on each of their three qualifying attempts.

Deborah Morton approached the beam unenthusiastically. Nobody had ever accused Debs of being faint of heart but the idea of preparing herself for a beating was extremely unappealing. She placed her hands along the wooden rail and halfheartedly leaned forward.

Patsy Butcher looked down the hall. Deborah was not yet in any position for receiving a running bender but she allowed her to remain leaning against the beam while she sent the remaining Red House gals to form a line along the back wall so that they were facing Deborah.

Yvonne and Janet bustled their way into poll position directly in front of Debs. They had the same shit-eating smirks on their faces that they had worn during the scolding. Deborah did her best to stare them down defiantly but their undisguised glee made her feel sick and humiliated.

She felt Patsy's hand on her shoulder. "I'm sorry Debs," the House Captain whispered, "But I'm going to need you to bend over as far as you can. I need you up as high as possible so that I can get a clean shot at you."

Deborah shot a bleak look at Patsy and then released her grip on the beam and reached her arms, head and upper torso down towards the floor.

Deborah's heart was pounding. For the third time since she had returned from furlough she was faced with the prospect of receiving twelve strokes. Debs was of the opinion that six was the perfect number for a caning. She accepted that three or even four strokes were probably not enough to punish a mega-minx of her experience. Six, on the other hand, she considered perfectly adequate. Just enough to keep steam coming out from under her bumbags for

Operation Scorched Arse

several hours, but not enough to distract her from going about her regular business. During her last extended beating Ms Lawton had broken the senior cane when delivering the tenth stroke and had been forced to complete the flogging with a prefect's ashplant. To compensate for using the lighter cane the Grand Dame had given Debs an additional two strokes. It had been the longest caning Deborah had ever received and she had been astonished by the exponential increase in the effect of each stroke the longer the punishment went on. She had no doubt that a twelve-stroke running bender from the athletic Patsy was going to be very tough duty indeed.

A Sound Beating

The remaining Red House gals watched in wide-eyed awe as Patsy sprinted down the long gymnasium.

There were only half a dozen gals in the hall who had ever been the recipients of running benders. Most of the gals, especially inmates in the early part of their sentences, had believed they were an urban legend spread about by the more experienced gals to spook them. But as the cane slashed across Deborah Morton's tautened bumbags the myth became an instant reality.

The voice over the public address system was unmistakable.

"One," announced Ms Lawton.

The gals in the gymnasium exchanged glances. They had always thought that the Grand Dame had eyes and ears everywhere but were baffled how she could be observing the proceedings in the gymnasium when she was nowhere to be seen.

Operation Scorched Arse

The gals on the landings looked startled. The crack of the cane exploding off Deborah Morton's bumbags had echoed through the building like a rifle shot.

During the walkthrough they had noticed Jackie Ivanhoe following behind the Debs and Cat parade. As Deborah was hustled out of the corridor and into the stairwell at the end of each landing Ivan would stoop down and prop open the door. The intent had eluded them until they heard the unmistakable sound of rattan ricocheting off gossamer.

Katie Beck grinned gleefully. She was seated in her office with the door open and she heard the sound of the caning cracking off Deborah's bumbags as clearly as if it was coming from next door in the Beak's study. She loved it when a plan came together.

Deborah Morton's head jerked back, her face contorted in agony. The past few days had not been kind to Deborah's rear end. In the space of less than a week she had been caned three times and all of the punishments had been from the top end of the spectrum. Even a whop-hardened veteran like Deborah was suffering from a touch of the residuals.

The cane had swiped across her slightly tender behind with the sting and venom of a rattle snake. When her eyes opened she was confronted by the gloating looks of Yvonne and Janet. She slumped back into a full hangover and panted in unexpurgated misery.

Patsy strode back down the gymnasium. She felt sorry for her victim but she had no choice other than to put her arm into the punishment. She had been horrified when the Grand Dame had told her that she wanted every stroke to be heard in all four corners of the building. Futilely she had objected and rewarded with a scathing lecture on Deborah's shortcomings and the Grand Dame had made thinly veiled threats regarding her own backside if Patsy failed to comply.

Patsy swooped down, the ceremonial house cane slicing through the air in a perfect arc and cutting across the very crown of Deborah's backside. By any standards it was a regal stroke and even Deb's sympathetic friends and fans couldn't help but be impressed by the sheer majesty of the manner in which the beating was being delivered.

The thwacks of the cane were music to Yvonne Godfrey and Janet Mitchell's ears. Every time Debs head reared back with her face contorted in agony the wicked prefects were filled with glee.

The cruel prefects had been delighted when Patty and Katie had summonsed them and outlined their new and most dastardly plan. Over the years Deborah had shown them nothing but contempt and they relished the idea of aiding and abetting in her public humiliation.

The whole plan had gone off swimmingly. Deborah had arrived in the library clearly prepared for a scrap. However, her pugnacious attitude had quickly evaporated and been replaced by incredulity when Patsy had explained the situation. Debs scored

Operation Scorched Arse

158 on the Cattell III B IQ test but for once she seemed to having considerable difficulty grasping the concepts being explained to her. Debs normal cocksure self-assurance seemed to elude her and a sheen of sweat had glistened on her brow as Patsy formally read out the charge.

Later, when the Wart explained the procedure for the Full Collar Walkthrough Deborah Morton had looked like she might burst into tears.

The cane exploded across Deborah's defenseless derriere forcing her head to snap back, her face contorted and her mouth formed into a silent howl.

Yvonne and Janet leered at her.

It had been Katie's idea to force the strokes to be heard all around the building.

"It'll stop Butcher from pulling the strokes," she advised the Wart, "and it'll give a whole new meaning to a sound beating."

"You are such a rotten bitch," the Wart had complimented Katie.

Anatomy of a Running Bender

A successful running bender requires precision timing and eye-cane coordination. Ideally the stroke will be delivered with the arm and cane in a perfect horizontal plane. Early or late execution of the stroke could result in miss-hits or fouls. Although Deborah was not in much of a position to be thankful while she was head down, arse up over the beam, she would be grateful later during the painful hours of recovery for Patsy's proficiency.

The members of the Red House watched in awe as Patsy sprinted down the gym. She had tied her waist-length braided dreadlocks back into a pony tail that swung from side to side as she accelerated. She swooped in low and sliced another perfect stripe across Deborah's behind.

"Six!" Ms Lawton announced over the loud speaker.
Patsy walked back up the library and looked at her watch.

Operation Scorched Arse

Deborah Morton was not having a good time of it. Patsy's careful accuracy meant that the first six strokes had all landed cleanly across the crown of her backside. There had been no wraparounds or high strikes which she was grateful for, but with a limited target area the House Captain was landing the strokes in close proximity to each other.

Deborah gritted her teeth. She knew that the next few minutes were going to be even more excruciating but she was determined not to howl or blub.

Patsy sighed and set off again down the center of the gym. The first time she had caned Deborah it had been a routine affair related to House Business. They had hugged afterwards and Deborah had complimented Patsy on her prowess and technique; telling her it was one of the better sixes she had ever received from a prefect. She hated having been forced to beat Deborah again but she was determined to deliver the thrashing with maximum force and minimum damage.

Patsy swooped in, the cane whistling through the air as she snapped her wrist with perfect timing. Debs left leg jerked backwards as the long stick slashed across the sweet spot.

"Seven," said Ms Lawton over the intercom.

Deborah was beginning to feel decidedly whop-weary. Her backside was on fire and she was completely helpless to defend herself. The manner in which she was positioned over the training beam meant she would need assistance to return to the vertical standing position. Her backside was sitting up proud for no other reason than to be thrashed with a thirty-six inch rattan cane.

Patsy tightened her grip on the ceremonial house cane. It was longer and thicker than the ashplant that she normally worked with, and compared favorably to the senior cane that Ms Lawton brandished with such aplomb. At the far end of the gymnasium Deborah was bent into a vee over the beam, her body supported by the balls of her feet, her heels off the ground and her gossamer covered backside sitting up perfectly. Patsy Butcher tapped the tip of the cane on the floor of the gymnasium and set off running.

Cathryn Cassidy sidled up beside Janet Mitchell. Mitch the Bitch was openly relishing Deborah's misfortune. Every time Debs head snapped back Janet's face split into an enormous grin. Cat Cassidy stamped her heel down on the bridge of Janet's foot. Mitch the Bitch squealed in anguish.

Deborah managed to suppress a squeal of anguish as the twelfth stroke sizzled across her backside. She felt Patsy leaning over her.
"Are you okay?" Patsy asked earnestly.
Debs grunted. "I'll live," she said through clenched teeth. "Just help me up."

Deborah received visits from well-wishers and sympathizers standing up. Rosemary had done her best to soothe her best chum's frazzled rump but Debs still felt as if she was sitting on a lighted griddle.

Operation Scorched Arse

The Bounder stopped by and slipped Debs several shots of vodka that helped a little but by the time bed-time came Deborah Morton was resigned to a long and painful night of lying face-down on her tummy.

With a double bare bender, a routine house beating, a public flogging and a Formal House Beating already under her bumbags it occurred to Debs that Ms Lawton was taking the business of declaring her Public Enemy Number One very seriously indeed.

Deborah Morton predicted she had some very hot and sweaty times ahead of her.

A Lunchtime Licking

Only hours after Deborah's appointment in the gymnasium the inmates got another insight into the inner workings of Operation Scorched Arse.

Rosemary Booker blushed ruefully as the Duty Monitor approached. She knew she was bang to rights and had no doubt that Yvonne Godfrey would have no hesitation in making the most out of the situation.

"I saw that Booker," Yvonne snapped, "In a hurry for lunch are you?"

"N..N..No... Well not really Godfrey, I'm sorry, I can go to the back of the queue if you want," Rosemary stammered.

"Oh sorry are we Booker?" Yvonne sneered. "You push in line bold as brass and now you're sorry."

Rosemary reddened slightly.

"You see the gal at the end of the line, Booker?"

Rosemary nodded.

Operation Scorched Arse

"Well you go outside and wait in the corridor and when that gal is sitting down I'm going to come and have a few words with you." With a sneer on her face Yvonne Godfrey reached into her pocket and theatrically produced her red card. There was a gasp in the hall. Queue jumping traditionally attracted a yellow card at worst. Most prefects would have let her off with a verbal warning.

"Booker, Phase 5," she announced loudly. "Six of the best for jumping line. Nose and toes in the corridor until I have time to deal with you."

With bowed head and a heavy tread Rosemary trudged out of the hall and into the corridor. Some of the gals in line gave her sympathetic grins but Rosemary was in no mood to return them. It was a long wait before the last gal had finally collected her lunch tray and made her way to her seat giving Rosemary plenty of time to ruminate on her latest misfortune.

Like most inmates of the facility Rosemary despised Yvonne Godfrey and had viewed her promotion to a member of the Elite with trepidation. Rosemary watched disconsolately as Yvonne entered the corridor. She had an uncomfortable feeling that she was about to get a humiliating scolding from the new prefect. Doubtless it would be delivered at one hundred decibels so everybody could hear.

However, Rosemary Booker was in for an even more unpleasant shock.

Yvonne Godfrey grinned wolfishly at Rosemary. "Hungry are we, Booker? Fancy some lunch now you've waited so long?"

"Oh yes, Godfrey, shall I cut along then?" Rosemary said hurriedly. Rosie couldn't believe her luck. Godders was letting her off.

Yvonne Godfrey continued to smile. "Yes Booker, you can cut along." Rosemary breathed a sigh of relief and started towards the door.

"But not just yet, Booker," Yvonne grinned, "I think we'd better have those whops first, wouldn't you agree."

Rosemary's glared at Yvonne. "Alright, Godfrey," she said quietly, "I know you want to break your duck so why don't we go up to the library and get it over with."

"That's the spirit Booker," Yvonne smiled, "but you're hungry and it seems such a waste of time traipsing all the way to the library, why don't we just deal with this here and now. Why don't you just go over there by the door and touch your toes?"

Rosemary stared at the prefect incredulously. "Whadaya you mean?" she managed to stutter.

"I would have thought it was quite clear, Booker," Yvonne said nonchalantly, "I want you to go over to the door, to bend over and to touch your toes."

Rosemary stared from the prefect to the open doorway, her mouth open in disbelief. It was unthinkable. To be caned in the open doorway would mean every gal in the lunch hall would hear.

Rosemary glared at Yvonne. "Yeah rock on Godders," she snarled.

"Go over to the door, bend over, touch them and get that big fat arse in the air where I can see it! Do I make myself clear, Booker, or do I need to call Ivan to hold you down?"

Operation Scorched Arse

Rosemary Booker looked at Godders contemptuously.

"You won't need to hold me down, you bitch," she hissed. "Lay it on thick as you like. You know it's only whops."

Rosemary Booker was the quietest member of the Famous Four. She was modestly studious, competently athletic and enjoyed playing modest parts in plays and productions. However, Rosemary excelled in an area that bemused even her closest chums. Her bum appeared impervious to pain. She seemed genuinely bemused after her first caning, "I don't understand what the fuss is about," she wondered, "it's only whops."

A Low-Rider

Rosemary turned and walked towards the doors of the cafeteria. Slowly she leant forward and reached down until her fingers rested on the tips of her pointed shoes. She waited while Yvonne rearranged her dress, turning back her skirt, exposing an enviable expanse of navy blue gossamer. Rosemary stared at a spot of wooden floor and tried her best to compose herself before the cane lashed across her drum tight bumbags. It was a scorcher, but Rosemary merely shifted her weight a little and then wriggled back into position

Yvonne Godfrey was enjoying herself. After six years as an inmate of the Back to School unit she had always dreamed of the day when she would finally assume the mantel of a member of the Elite. It had always struck Yvonne Godfrey that being on the end other than the receiving end of the cane would be very good duty indeed.

For several years Yvonne had been making covert plans with Patty Hodge and Katie Beck that

Operation Scorched Arse

once she was finally installed in the Elite she would establish the most heinous incarnation of the Secret Sorority of Serial Spankers in the units history. Yvonne Godfrey would act as Commandant of the fearsome SS and would enjoy the full protection of the Radical Right. Yvonne was delighted that she was able to open her open her whop account across the trophy bumbags of one of the unit's most beloved legends. She was certain that Patty would approve.

Yvonne stared at the sea of gossamer with a glint of relish in her eye. She whipped the cane down and grinned as it sent the full moons wiggling and jiggling. She stepped in again and let loose another scorcher. She was disappointed that Rosemary wasn't showing some reaction by now; she would dearly enjoy observing the unfortunate inmate demonstrate her discomfort.

Down below Rosemary was standing her ground stoically. Despite Godders best efforts Rosie was unperturbed by the assault on her bumbags except for the ignominy of being punished so publicly.

Yvonne Godfrey gripped the cane tightly and stepped in for the fifth time. She stooped down and lashed the cane on the soft sulcus of the voluptuous orbs. For the first time Rosemary hissed with consternation. Even the apparently whop-insensate Rosie was not completely insensitive to low-riders.
Although the delivery of low-riders was officially frowned upon and discouraged, it was generally accepted that an occasional miss-hit was going to occur in the cut and thrust of a whopping.

Yvonne grinned to herself, the slice across the sulcus had been far from a miss-hit, she had clinically taken aim and fired off a perfect shot, right on the money.

As Yvonne took aim, both gals were fully aware they were about to enter the final battle of wills. Rosemary Booker, a veteran with over a hundred canings already under her skirt, knew that the last stroke would be the hottest, ripest, spiciest stripe of six sizzling strokes. Yvonne Godfrey knew that it was her last chance to make Rosemary squeal.

The cane cut across Rosemary's bumbags with a crack that echoed around the lunch hall. Every gal in the hall winced. Rosemary blinked.

For a moment she didn't move then slowly she rose to her feet. She pushed her skirt down and turned silently to face her nemesis. The two gals eyes met and to Yvonne's chagrin Rosemary smiled at her.

Yvonne stood, smoking rod in hand, bitterly disappointed not to have gotten more reaction out of her victim. Still, she consoled herself, Rosemary was only the first gal she had licked so far and there would be plenty more fish to fry.

Yvonne poked Rosemary in the chest with the tip of her ashplant.

"Get your fat arse in there and get some lunch, Booker," she said unpleasantly. "When you've finished bring me your punishment book so we can deal with the post-processing. You can tell me how it was."

Rosemary glared at Yvonne. "It was barely warm, that's how it was," she said tartly. "If that's the best you've got to dish out then we don't have anything to worry about."

Yvonne just grinned. "You know and I know that's not true. Why don't you go and sit down and see how you enjoy that low-rider rubbing against the chair."

Rosemary snorted disparagingly and stomped back into the cafeteria.

"Fucking bitch," groaned Rosemary as she took her place next to her chums. "That low-rider was intentional."

Jojo patted Rosie's hand sympathetically.

"She's mean and rotten to the core," Nixdown snorted. "You should have hacked her in the shins. These Radical Revisions are beginning to give me the pip."

"I think we're only just seeing the tip of the iceberg," predicted Jojo ominously.

Surprise, Surprise!

The Famous Four were not having a good day of it. Later that evening Jojo and Nixdown were taken by surprise.

"You what?" snapped Nicola Jane Nixon.

Jennifer Gardiner took a sharp step back. Nix looked as if she might cuff the Little Brat around the ear, or worse still hack her on the shins.

"I'm sorry Nixon," said the grubby nervously, as she thrust the red envelopes forward. "I'm just the messenger."

Jojo stepped between her chum and the nervous Brat. "It's okay Jenny," she said soothingly, "I'll take those." She reached over and took the envelopes. "Cut along now," she said comfortingly, "you ain't done nothing wrong."

Jennifer Gardiner breathed an audible sigh of relief and cut along. Very sharpish.

Jojo looked at Nixdown and sighed. Her best chum's pretty features had been rearranged into a sullen pout. She stood with her hands on her hips looking obstinate. Jojo knew the look all too well.

Operation Scorched Arse

"We'd better cut along," Joanna said pragmatically, "lets get it over with."

"Cut along my arse," growled Nix. "I ain't cutting along anywhere."

Jojo sighed. "What are you going to do? Do a bunk? Where is that going to get you?"

"I'm going for a fag," said Nix and stomped off.

Jojo hurried after her. "Ok already," she laughed. "But, just one."

"What's this all about, Evans?" Nix asked pugnaciously.

Penelope Ann Evans looked sympathetic. "Well, you've both got five red marks for rubbishing the pre's, so you're going to be dangled", she said quietly.

"Dangled?" exploded Nix. "You haven't got any authority to dangle us; we're in Phase Five now!"

"I'm afraid you're wrong Nixon," Penelope Ann informed them. "Read the new protocols."

"Oh for gawd's sake," groaned Nixdown.

"New protocols or no new protocols," interjected Jojo, "how can we have five red marks, we've only been back a week?"

Penelope Ann sighed. "You both had four at the end of last year," she explained.

"Last year? What the fuck has last year got to do with the price of whops?" snapped Nix. "You know as well as I do that the slate's wiped clean at the end of each term."

"Not any more. The new protocols say that hangovers will apply."

"Oh my giddy aunt," laughed Jojo, "this is just so bogus."

Joanna Heyworth was by far the most dangled gal in the facility. She refused to be intimidated by the Serial Spankers and treated the more pompous and prissy factions of the Elite with disdain.

Although rubbishing pre's could be a delightful recreation it had a painful downside.

The process of issuing red marks was covert and obscure. On the wall of the Elite common room there was a card index system, with an individual card for every inmate at the facility. If a prefect felt that she had been rubbished she would take the gals card and annotate it in red ink. When a gal reached four annotations her card would be moved to an area of the index system known as the 'Hot Zone'. If a prefect felt a gal in the Hot Zone had rubbished her, she would annotate her card and place it in a red envelope. She would then notify the Red-shirt who would send her personal grubby to seek out the inmate and have her cut along sharpish to the library.

Rubbishing was a poorly defined term and the prefects were free to interpret it as they felt fit. If they personally caned an inmate they were forced to state the reason in the gal's Punishment Record Book and file a report with Patty Hodge. However, if they just didn't like the way an inmate looked at them or any other imagined slur that they would have difficulty explaining they took recourse by issuing red marks. Rubbishing abuse was rampant, especially amongst the members of the Secret Sorority of Serial Spankers, better known as the SS, who would conspire to target particular inmates. Any gal unfortunate enough to land in the Hot Zone was guaranteed to suffer a dangling within days.

Operation Scorched Arse

Jojo's overt disdain for the SS meant she was a regular resident in the Hot Zone.

Katie Beck's tenure as Red-shirt had left many unpleasant legacies for the Woody gals to suffer. Having caned every gal at the unit she complained to the Grand Dame that the thin whippy ashplant was not an appropriate instrument for whipping the whop-hardened arses of the likes of April Turner, Cathryn Cassidy, Melanie White or Lady Victoria. Ms Lawton approved the use of a long handled, oval headed, wood backed brush which proved significantly more punishing.

Next Katie procured an oversized stool from a local antique shop. To the dismay of her victims the stool had no side bars for them to hold on to and the extreme height of the stool meant that once that they were over and up they were literally dangling with their hands and feet unable to reach the floor.

Six well-placed cracks of the brush could pretty well color a gal's bum red from the top to bottom of each cheek. Being dangled was considered very bad duty indeed by the inmates of the Back to School unit.

Nailing the Big BUTT

Penelope Ann Evans was a statuesque gal and looked magnificent in the red shirt and black tie that signified her office. She helped Joanna up and over her lap and rearranged Jojo's clothing. Once she had Jojo tucked in tightly and her bottom bared, Penny unfastened the cuff button of her blouse and rolled up her right sleeve.

Penelope Ann and Jojo were tight. Their equestrian careers went back years and they were hoping that their application to allow the Woody riding team to compete in the national trials would soon be approved. Penny Ann was uncomfortable with many of the radical revisions to the protocols but nonetheless she was duty bound to impose them. She raised the hairbrush to shoulder height then brought it down with a crack.

Jojo was completely reliant on Penelope Ann for support, her arms and legs dangled down on either side without any hope of reaching the floor. The new Red-shirt was demonstrating considerable

Operation Scorched Arse

skill with the hairbrush and by the time the sixth spank slapped across Jojo's lower left cheek the reigning Big BUTT considered herself to be well and truly spanked. Hanging upside down, panting for breath Jojo waited for Penelope Ann to help her back into the vertical position.

"Holy Fuck," yelped Jojo. The seventh whap had caught her completely unprepared.

Nixdown turned her face away from the wall and gaped. In four years she had never heard Jojo utter as much as a moan or a groan under the numerous assaults that her derriere had endured. But as the eighth slap cracked down Jojo was showing some considerable signs of consternation. Her legs were kicking frantically and her head was shaking.

"Jesus H," thought Nixdown, "she's fucking nailed Jojo."

Penelope Ann Evans took a tight hold around Jojo's waist and tucked her in closely. Penny had been an unlikely selection as Red-shirt; she was quiet and unassuming and was generally happier in the company of her pony than her fellow inmates. Nonetheless when the baton had been passed to her she was determined to take it up and prove herself.

However, she was flabbergasted to find that with her first outing with the Red-shirt's hairbrush she had nailed the unit's toughest nut to crack.

"Jesus H," she thought to herself, "I've fucking nailed Jojo!"

Joanna Heyworth desperately tried to compose herself. The extra slaps of the brush had caught her unawares and had sent her central nervous system into momentary confusion. She had been mentally prepared for six and had put it up and kept it up without complaint. When the sixth smack had blistered her bum she had felt the familiar feeling of rueful relief. It was hot, it was sweaty, but it was over. It was hardly cricket to unleash an unannounced seventh slap on a gal who was only expecting six.

"Jesus H," thought Jojo, "she's fucking nailed me!"

Nicola Jane Nixon turned back to the wall and pressed her nose against the wood paneling. Behind her the dangling was continuing unabated, she heard a ninth slap and then a tenth. Nicola Jane began to mutter her indecipherable Nixdown hexes as she continued to press her nose to the wall.

The Radical Reforms to the protocols were really beginning to give her the pip.

Penelope Ann helped Jojo slide back down to her feet. Jojo rummaged under her skirt, rearranging her bumbag elastic and straightening her blouse tails. She smoothed down her skirt and fiddled with her tie before retrieving her blazer.

"You okay?" asked Penny.

Jojo looked at her straight in the eye. "You nailed me because you took me by surprise," she said bluntly. "It won't happen again."

Nonetheless, Joanna thought to herself, the new protocols clearly did not bode well for the future of her backside.

Operation Scorched Arse

Nixdown peeled off her blazer and set it aside. She stepped over to the spanking stool and offered her wrist to Penelope Ann so she could be assisted over and up.

She felt the hem of her skirt being turned back and the tails of her blouse being moved out of the firing line. She gritted her teeth as she felt the back of the brush circling on her naked flesh.

Unappealing as the prospect of a double dangling might be at least she had the advantage of knowing what to expect.

"Go ahead Evans, hot as you like," she said through clenched teeth, "but don't think that you're gonna nail me, 'cos you won't."

Penny Ann raised the hairbrush and brought it crashing down.

The Fabulous Fart

Before the week was out Deborah Morton received another tough lesson in exactly how hard life could be when you had been declared Public Enemy Number One at the nation's most austere Back to School unit. Midway through a music tutorial Ms Whitton bent her over the piano stool and beat her with a violin bow.

"Morton, fetch the violin bow and step up!" snapped Ms Whitton, who acted as the Music Dame around the facility.

As she trudged towards the front of the room Deborah Morton had good reason to be alarmed.

For the first few years as an inmate at the facility Debs had been Ms Whitton's star pupil. Her exceptional talent as a clarinetist and her fine singing voice had won her considerable favor with the Music Dame. However, fatefully that favored relationship would all change with a sound of another nature altogether.

Operation Scorched Arse

During the autumn term of Deborah's fourth year at the facility, the early rehearsals of the upcoming Woodys Christmas production of Handel's Messiah were progressing extremely well. Ms Whitton smiled to herself as she guided the choir into the beginning of the Hallelujah chorus. She was particularly fond of the piece and had taken inordinate time and care over the arrangement.

Ms Whitton turned to lead in the altos. As the choristers began to sing she was surprised to notice that Deborah Morton had missed the beat. Thinking it to merely be an uncharacteristic error from her musical star she turned away, but moments later when she turned her attention back to the altos she was aghast to see that Deborah was not only not singing at all, but appeared to be engrossed in reading something she had extracted from her blazer pocket.

Angrily the music instructor indicated to the choir to stop.

"Morton," she barked. "Step up before the choir this minute."

Deborah was jolted to her senses and hurriedly stuffed the paper back into her pocket. Slightly red faced she made her way up before the enraged Dame.

"You're not singing, gal" Ms Whitton snapped. "Explain yourself immediately."

It would have been an easy matter for Deborah to have made up an excuse that she had a sore throat and didn't want to strain herself, but instead what followed would earn Debs a place in the annals of Woody lore forever.

With perfect comic timing Deborah Morton farted.

It was not a small, secretive girly grunt but an enormous fart. Enough wind to make a gals skirt flap and to strain the seams of her bumbags. It was flatulence on a fantastic scale. It was a fart that swooped and soared and echoed throughout the hall.

T'was a veritably gargantuan guff.

For a moment the hall was quiet. Then Deborah Morton began to laugh. She rocked back on her heels and tickled her ribs with mirth. She was quickly accompanied by the hysterical tittering of the rest of the choir as they celebrated the sheer majesty of the fabulous fart.

Momentarily Ms Whitton stared at Deborah Morton, an incredulous look on her face. For a hefty lady she moved with remarkable speed. She grabbed Deborah Morton by the wrist and in a fluid movement sat back on the piano stool and dumped the helpless inmate face down over her knee. With even greater speed she had turned back Deborah's skirt and to the amazement of the assembled choir she yanked Deborah's bumbags down until they were concertinaed around her ankles.

At first Deborah had been winded by her dizzying downward journey but she quickly regained her breath and started to struggle. However, fit and athletic though she was, Deborah was no match for the brawny Dame.

"Leggo of me," Deborah wailed, "Lemme up!"

Operation Scorched Arse

The indignity of having her bare bottom displayed to the choir was just too ghastly and Deborah kicked and struggled and squirmed with all her strength.

"Lemme go you bitch!" she screamed.

Ms Whitton had a tight hold on the squirming inmate and an even firmer hold on the conductor's baton, which she had raised high in the air. She brought the baton down with terrific force.

A Bare Bum Spanking

"Lemme go I tell you," Deborah wailed as the baton flailed at her naked bottom. The baton rose and fell with startling speed. Deborah Morton vainly tried to escape from Ms Whitton's vice-like grip but the Dame just kept on whacking. After six whacks Ms Whitton showed no inclination to stop, after a dozen she merely seemed to be warming to her work, and the blows continued to rain down.

Deborah Morton was no newcomer to having her butt whipped, but this was a thrashing without precedent. Deborah's legs were kicking frantically; her body was twisting, her head shaking violently and Deborah Morton, amongst the toughest gals at the unit, started to howl.

The authority to administer punishment to the bare bottom was limited to the Grand Dame and the Red-shirt. Members of the Brass were strictly limited to administering six strokes during any single punishment. However, Ms Whitton seemed oblivious to these rules, her arm pumped up and down and Deborah's bottom was being slashed to tatters. The

Operation Scorched Arse

skinny baton was only a light implement but administered with such purpose made it an instrument of stinging torment.

By now Deborah's howls were changing from indignation to genuine distress. The baton continued to slice across her arse and the frenzied Dame was showing no signs of letting up. Deborah's cheeks were criss-crossed with angry weals and her struggles were becoming frantic. Her legs scissored through the air, her buttocks squirmed and wriggled to escape the onslaught, she tried to put her hands back to protect herself to no avail, but still the beating continued.

The members of the choir watched in horrified awe. Ms Whitton was thrashing Deborah with the fervor of a frenzied zealot. Her arm was pumping up and down at a frantic pace.

Debs Morton had a reputation for inspiring ire in members of the Brass and the Elite but even by her unfortunate standards the untimely release of wind had pushed Ms Whitton over the brink. It appeared to the choristers that she was literally frothing at the mouth.

Finally after the baton had slashed across Deborah's backside three dozen times or more Ms Whitton began to slow down. With three last swipes the whipping finally drew to a close.

The hall was suddenly silent. Ms Whitton dragged up Deborah's bumbags and smoothed down her skirt. Debs remained sprawled across the Dame's lap as if uncertain of what to do. Roughly Ms Whitton yanked Deborah to her feet. Debs, normally so self-assured, stood in front of the choir with her head bowed looking shell-shocked.

Ms Whitton pointed to the door. "Get out of my sight," she snarled, and with a heavy tread Deborah Morton left the hall, tears trickling down her cheeks.

There was an enquiry of course; Deborah was given the opportunity to report the matter to her Court Appointed Guardian and to file a complaint. However, she knew that if she filed a complaint it would become a matter of public record. Four years earlier she had suffered the humiliation of her public arrest and the subsequent castigation in the press. Debs Morton was less than enthusiastic about returning to the public eye in relation to a fart, fabulous or otherwise. She elected to keep Woody business as Woody business. Ms Whitton was given a six-month ban from beating Deborah.

During the six months that followed the incident of the Fabulous Fart Ms Whitton sent Deborah to Coventry, limiting their relationship strictly to choir and orchestra business.

However, the night that Ms Lawton announced the implementation of Operation Scorched Arse and branded Debs as Public Enemy Number One was coincident with the end of the ban period. The Grand Dame took the music instructor to one side.

"Your thrashing rights over Deborah Morton have been fully reinstated," the Grand Dame informed Ms Whitton. "I'm sure should the opportunity arise you will do the right thing."

"Yes, Grand Dame," grinned Ms Whitton. "It will be my pleasure."

Operation Scorched Arse

"But one thing, Ms Whitton," said the Grand Dame. "Everything must appear one hundred per cent legitimate."

"Of course Ma'am," smiled the Dame, "I'll take care of everything."

12

Bacon Slicers

Ms Whitton was considered to be a power-beater. She was large framed and extremely strong. She didn't punish gals with the prolificacy of Patty Hodge, the Wart or Katie Beck but on the occasions she did choose to wield the violin bow the events were memorable.

Deborah Morton was stretched out across the piano stool with her bumbags sitting up proud. Above her the music instructor had the violin bow raised above her head. The low lie of the stool meant that by the time the tip of the bow reached its target it was moving at terminal velocity.

Deborah's chums watched sympathetically. It was evident to everybody in the room that this was not a regular punishment. Ms Whitton was swiping the bow down with all her might, the sound of the wooden stick rebounding off Deborah's bumbags literally echoed around the room.

The bow whistled through the air, colliding with Deborah's defenseless bottom with unmitigated force. Debs bucked and wriggled and kicked. Her chums watched anxiously as Ms Whitton prepared for the last and probably most formidable swipe.

"Get up gal!" snapped Ms Whitton.

Deborah couldn't believe her ears. The Dame must have miscounted. She was going to get off with five. Painfully she pushed herself up and smoothed her skirt down. Stiff-legged she slowly started back towards her desk.

"Where do you think you're going?" barked the Dame.

Deborah turned and looked plaintively at Ms Whitton.

"Bend over," the Dame snapped.

Deborah grimaced.

"Turn around Morton and bend over and touch your toes."

Slowly Deborah turned and faced the seated inmates. She bent forward at the waist and reached down towards the tips of her shoes. Ms Whitton turned back the hem of her skirt.

The tension in the room was palpable. They watched Ms Whitton take careful aim, raise the violin bow in the air then slice it downwards. Involuntarily Deborah stood bolt upright her hands clasping at her cheeks, a look of anguish on her face. It was a perfectly executed bacon slicer.

Ms Whitton tapped the floor in front of Deborah's shoes.

"Touch them Morton," she snapped, "you know the form."

With trembling fingers Deborah reached down.

Bacon slicing was a highly specialized technique. Instead of swiping the cane across the buttocks horizontally it was brought down vertically, aiming to make only the slightest contact. When executed perfectly it made a gal feel as if a layer of flesh had been sliced off. The sensation was short lived but instantly agonizing.

Ms Whitton slashed down a second perfectly executed bacon slicer. This time Deborah's shoulders jolted back and her fingers raised six inches from her shoes. Despite her anguish she pushed forward and got her fingers back in place. She could hardly hold back the tears.

"Stay down," ordered Ms Whitton.

"That ain't fair!" growled Nicola Jane at the back of the room.

"Silence! Silence in the room!" bellowed Ms Whitton.

She slashed the violin bow down. For the third time Debs jerked up.

At the back of the room Jojo, Nix and Rosemary watched in horror. Debs fingers had hardly left her toes for a second but still the music instructor was calling it as a bad strike. Technically the protocols said that if a gal was touching her toes during punishment then she should not rise from position until given permission. However, even the harshest of Dames realized that the toe-touching position was extremely difficult to maintain and if a gal recovered her stance promptly the strike was called good. Ms Whitton was using the most ruthless interpretation of the protocols possible. Deborah only had two

Operation Scorched Arse

chances. She either had to stay down so that the six was complete or otherwise Ms Whitton had to miss.

The violin bow slashed down perfectly. The pain was almost insurmountable but somehow Deborah found the will to keep her fingers on her toes. Ms Whitton looked furious, but she had no choice, the beating was finally street legal.

"Get up gal," she snarled. "Go back to your desk and stand on your chair with your hands on your head for the remainder of this tutorial."

The New SS

Yvonne Godfrey and her cronies were in hog heaven. The imposition of zero-tolerance and Operation Scorched Arse had made them feel omnipotent. Almost daily some poor gal would be publicly red carded, then collared and marched through the facility. Up in the library she would have her bumbags cut to tatters by one or the other of the Secret Sorority of Serial Spankers. The new SS had worked on enhancing many of Katie Beck's original forms of torture. They used the burly prefect Jackie Ivanhoe as their enforcer. She quickly earned the nickname of Ivan the Terrible. Ivan towered head and shoulders over most of the inmates and used her physique to make collaring even more heinous than before. She would raise gals up onto tiptoes and pin their arms up behind their backs, occasionally spitefully giving them Chinese burns into the bargain as she hustled them through the facility.

Abuse of the rubbishing regulations was out of control. Yvonne and her cohorts played a cunning

Operation Scorched Arse

game. To ensure that they didn't attract attention to themselves they were careful to make sure that reports of rubbishing were spread out between them. The Red-shirt, Penelope Ann Evans soon found that she was dangling two or three gals a day.

Penelope Ann despised the SS. The Elite was split into two factions: the dreaded SS, and the Red-shirt and her lieutenants, Cathryn Cassidy, Melanie White and the Butcher Twins, who did their best to keep Yvonne in check. Penelope Ann raised her suspicions of Yvonne's manipulation of the rules and regulations with Ms Hodge but the Deputy Grand Dame told her that she would do nothing without hard evidence and forbade the Red-shirt from bringing the matter up with Ms Lawton.

Patty and her cohorts on the Radical Right had spent years covertly training Yvonne Godfrey for the job, laying out plans and molding her to command the most heinous team of Serial Spankers in the units history.

Patty's original plan was to install Yvonne in the role of Red-shirt with Janet Mitchell as her deputy. However, even Patty conceded that this would not be an easy sell. Yvonne was extremely unpopular both with the inmates and the majority of the Brass. Nonetheless, Patty campaigned diligently and lobbied Ms Lawton with pro-Godders speeches at every opportunity.

Patty's plans took a setback when Dotty Hammell, the leader of the Liberal Left proposed Cathryn Cassidy as an alternative.

Patty was apoplectic. She loathed Cathryn. They had a history pre-dating the Back to School unit.

Cathryn had attended the exclusive Dartington Manor School where Patty Hodge was employed as the Mistress in Charge of Discipline. Patty had singled Cathryn out as a subversive and thrashed her frequently with her infamous wye-tipped canes. Cat had treated Patty with the utmost contempt and continued to subvert to her hearts content.

With Cathryn in charge of the Elite Patty feared that her plans for the new SS would be thwarted. Despite her haughty and arrogant demeanor Yvonne was a typical bully and was unlikely to be prepared to go toe-to-toe with someone as forceful as Cat.

Patty immediately embarked on a hostile anti-Cat campaign, constantly reminding the Grand Dame that it was Cathryn who had authored the *'Manifesto for Mega-minxdom'* and founded the troublesome cult.

Patty had a problem. The outgoing Red-shirt was none other than April Turner. Many Woody historians cite April as the original mega-minx and the inspiration for Cathryn's manifesto. Nonetheless, Ms Lawton had decided to experiment and selected April to fill the unit's most prestigious position. The experiment had been hailed as a resounding success.

Dotty and her liberal friends seemed to be edging ahead and Cat looked set for the Red-shirt when Patty unexpectedly changed horses.

Patty selected Penelope Ann Evans as her new candidate. It was a masterful move. Penny Ann was a quiet and uncontroversial member of the community. Patty figured that she was the perfect alternative to the arrogant Yvonne and the wayward Cat.

Penelope Ann was dismayed to suddenly find herself thrust into the race. She was shy and reserved by nature. She preferred to spend her time quietly in the stables tending to her horse. She had no desire to be thrust into the hectic life-style of acting as Redshirt. Nonetheless, when the time came to vote the Radical Right and the Liberal Left concurred and she was appointed with a hefty majority.

Yvonne was deeply aggrieved by what she interpreted as Patty's betrayal but the Deputy Grand Dame placated her.

"Penny Ann will be a lame duck," she promised. "You'll be able to operate with impunity and Cassidy won't be able to interfere. This is going to be a great year for the SS."

Caning Prefects

Despite her promises to Yvonne Patty remained concerned about Cathryn. Even though she wasn't physically wearing the Red-shirt she was still a force to be reckoned with. After a long night plotting with Katie and the Wart in the saloon bar of the Bunch of Grapes Patty came up with a cunning plan.

As Deputy Grand Dame, Patricia Hodge was responsible for overseeing the performance and behavior of the Elite. She pored over the Radical Reforms to the rules, regulations and protocols that Ms Lawton had implemented until she found a chink.

According to the protocols the Elite were treated differently to the other inmates. The Elite Code of Discipline dictated that the only member of staff authorized to cane a prefect was the Grand Dame herself. Prefects sent up to the Principal's study received mandatory double bare benders. Caning of prefects was relatively rare as the code offered them considerable protection.

Operation Scorched Arse

The code was especially favorable to the members of the Elite with regard to misconduct during lectures and tutorials. It stated that a prefect could only be red-carded out of lectures for causing a *material* disruption to the proceedings and required considerable paperwork to support the application for a beating. The Brass could rarely be bothered with the hassle.

Patricia Hodge called a meeting of the Radical Right. She instructed her cohorts to file a series of complaints against Cathryn and her chums for creating minor disturbances that went unpunished. In the meantime Patty promised she would draft a white-paper on prefectorial misconduct titled *'Elite Beating : Public or Private?'*

With fortuitous timing Ms Hodge delivered the white paper just as Ms Lawton had decided to unleash the full force of Operation Scorched Arse on the inmates. Barely giving the document a second glance Ms Lawton curtly told her deputy to revise the protocols as appropriate and to implement whatever policies she deemed necessary.

Patty commissioned the Wart to perform the first ever caning of a prefect in a lecture room. Predictably her target was Cathryn Cassidy. It was not as successful as Patty had hoped. Cathryn did not appear the least bit fazed by the punishment. However, Patty was not a woman to be deterred. She gathered her cronies and announced the next phase of her plan. The Radical Right was instructed to embark on a program of Elite Beatings with Cathryn and her closest chums, Melanie White and the Butcher Twins as the specified targets.

Shortly the sound of rattan rattling off tautened gossamer in the Elite lecture rooms became commonplace.

Yvonne Godfrey was furious. "You're supposed to protect us," she complained bitterly to Patty. "That stupid bitch put me over her knee and spanked me with a wooden spoon."

Patty sighed. Despite her efforts to restrict the program of prefectorial beatings to Cathryn and her three chums the Liberal Left were not playing ball. She had already received complaints from several members of the SS that they had been forced to bend over in the lecture rooms and now Dotty Hammell had had the audacity to spank Patty's commandant.

"I'll speak to everybody involved and make sure it never happens again," Patty assured Yvonne.

Patty did not find Dotty very receptive.

"You made the rules, Patricia," the Domestic Science Dame retorted when Patty scolded her for spanking Yvonne. "Godfrey backgabbed at me so I spanked her just the same as I would have had it been anybody else."

"But I gave her my word," said Patty lamely.

"Too bad," said Dotty emphatically. "You'd better tell little Miss Godfrey that if she doesn't want to be spanked she'd better keep that crabby tongue of hers in her mouth."

Patty didn't have any more luck with Pauline Gascoigne, Stephanie Powell or Jane Lummell. They

Operation Scorched Arse

were all adamant; if the gloves were off with the Elite then the SS was fair game.

Patty Hodge scowled and growled dark mutterings and wondered how she should break the news to Yvonne.

Scorched Arses

The sound of canes rebounding off tautened gossamer reverberated around the campus morning, noon and night as the zero-tolerance policy was strictly imposed. The whop rate was increasing in every aspect of the inmates lives.

Katie zealously enforced the Politics of Clobber. Every morning there was a queue outside her door of inmates waiting for their circulation to be kick-started with Katie's leather soled slipper.

The no gabbing or goofing in assembly protocol was gleefully imposed by members of the SS responsible for monitoring the hall. Red cards were at a premium.

In the lecture rooms the standard modus operandi of issuing verbal warnings and yellow cards prior to resorting to corporal punishment was largely a thing of the past. The Radical Right were particularly ruthless, but even the darlings on the Liberal Left were using the cane with increased regularity.

Operation Scorched Arse

Free-time was fraught with danger for the inmates. Outside the hours they spent in the lecture rooms the facility was pre-dominantly administered by the Elite. Despite Penny Ann's efforts to control them Yvonne and her SS prowled the corridors and recreation areas looking for signs of mischief and malfeasance. They would swoop down on hapless inmates and after securing them in a full collar haul them off to the library.

Patty took to making spot checks to ensure that Melanie White wasn't cutting any slack during Dorm Raids. Melanie would often arrive on a landing to find that the Deputy Grand Dame already had several inmates bending over their beds waiting to be caned.

Sporting spanking had reached epic proportions. Misguidedly Penelope Ann had acceded to Ms Hodge's advice to select Juliet Spage to act as the Senior Brat Draper. In her role Juliet was responsible for overseeing the Brat mentoring programs and was at liberty to drape all or any of the twelve newest inmates whenever she felt that they were falling short of performance expectations. Apparently Juliet's expectations were high and performance was low as she found grounds for spanking a minimum of a Brat a day. Penelope Ann again vainly tried to intervene but as usual Ms Hodge refused to listen and admonished her harshly for her liberal opinions.

Katie Beck pulled off a major coup when she persuaded Ms Lawton to allow her to stage an impromptu clobber stand-down. The inmates were startled to hear an instruction come over the public announcement system for them to, "Stand to attention, hands on your heads, standby for a full clobber inspection."

Katie had timed the stand-down for afternoon break when all of the inmates were outside in the recreation area getting some fresh air.

"Clobber abuse is rampant," she explained. "I slippered six gals this morning. It's time we sent out a stronger message. We'll stage an impromptu stand-down and we'll find tons of abuse. It will teach them a damn good lesson."

Katie Beck and Ms Hodge scrupulously inspected every gal in the recreation area. First their blazers were inspected for loose threads and stains. Ms Lawton had given a single dispensation, that the gals would not be punished for stray hairs that might be found on their blazers. After her blazer had been inspected the gal was instructed to remove her jacket and fold it at her feet. Next, she was told to put her tie over her shoulder, lowering the bib of her gymslip if necessary, and return her hands onto the top of her head.

Katie was familiar with every nuance of the protocols regarding clobber and almost immediately the slipperings commenced.

To the horror of the inmates they discovered that if they were found to have a dangling thread on a button or loose stitching on her collar braiding they were told to bend over and slippered right there in the recreation area.

Belinda Lee, whose notorious lack of clobber control had earned her the nickname of the Scruff, had so many uniform infractions that after she was soundly slippered by Ms Hodge, she was sent up to

Operation Scorched Arse

Ms Lawton for a bare bender. Rosemary Booker, another inmate with considerable clobber challenges also visited the Grand Dame. By the time inspection was over twenty-three inmates had been slippered in the recreation area.

The inmates of the facility were not best impressed by this new turn of events. Katie and Patty on the other hand celebrated the first ever mass slippering late into the night.

These were hot and sweaty times for the mega-minxes.

Anarchy and Chaos

However, far from being cowed into submission the mega-minxes retaliated by embarking upon a rampage of mischief and mayhem. Japing the Brass and rubbishing the pre's was the order of the day.

Ms Lawton observed the escalation of anarchy and chaos with increasing dismay. During the summer, when she had first drafted the Radical Revisions, she had intended them as a short-term response to the seemingly unstoppable rise in mischief and malfeasance that had permeated through the community during the previous twelve months. She figured that the imposition of the zero-tolerance policy code-named Operation Scorched Arse would act as a deterrent and help to restore a modicum of order.

It had been a calculated decision but the Grand Dame was beginning to acknowledge that it might have back-fired.

Operation Scorched Arse

The escalation in the whop rate was not limited to the twelve most notorious mega-minxes that she had branded the Dirty Dozen and denounced as hostiles. Inmates who had previously been content to watch the shenanigans from the sidelines were signing up to the cult of mega-minxdom in droves. Gals who had previously only accumulated a handful of punishments each year were establishing new personal records. Mischief and mayhem prevailed despite the inmate's knowledge that their behavior would inevitably conclude with them contracting a dose of scorched arse syndrome.

Ms Lawton was in a dilemma. Although Operation Scorched Arse was not turning out as planned it would be difficult to change course. With so many new recruits to the subversive cult she had no logical evidence that a relaxation of the zero-tolerance policy would have any positive effect.

Ms Lawton reviewed the latest sheaf of papers that Katie had left on her desk. The pages contained Patty Hodge's most recent proposals for revisions to the wording of various rules, regulations and protocols.

She drummed her fingers on her desk. The amendments were subtle but the Grand Dame knew that every altered nuance was designed to make life even harder for the inmates.

"The whop rate is rising satisfactorily," Patty reported. "We're up almost fifty per cent from this time last year. Even the damn liberals are whopping up a storm. Zero-tolerance is certainly the way forward. Have you signed the new amendments yet? I think that they'll really make a difference."

Ms Lawton looked thoughtful. "Patricia do you remember the time when we were at school and you thrashed me on suspicion of malfeasance? You told me it was for my own good. I thought it was rather harsh and complained so you put me over your knee and spanked me for being cheeky. Do you remember that?"

Patty reached over and patted the Grand Dames hand. "Now, now, Susan," she said unctuously. "I thought that we'd agreed to let sleeping dogs lie. You know that I've always accepted your authority as Grand Dame and I've done everything I can to support you. There's no point in dwelling on a few whops from the past. Besides what did they always tell us? Gals are born broad of beam and designed for a good tight six of the best?"

"How many inmates have been caned today?" asked Ms Lawton.

"Well I'd need to check the record, but at least half a dozen," responded Patty.

"That's quite a lot of sixes," mused Ms Lawton.

"Actually it should have been more," said Patty. "If you just sign these adjustments to the protocols it will stop those damn liberals handing out yellow cards instead of reds. We would have scored at least three more sets of whops if you had signed the amendments when I sent them to you. Now, I'm not trying to tell you how to do your job, Susan, but we still have considerable work to do. It's anarchy and chaos out there and all we have to respond with is the policy of zero-tolerance. This is no time to be lily-livered."

Operation Scorched Arse

"I've finished a complete re-write of the Politics of Clobber," Katie told the Grand Dame enthusiastically. "I've tightened up a lot of clauses so that those damn liberals will be forced to quit cutting slack. I've reclassified some elements to zero-tolerance. I'm expecting a substantial improvement in the whop-rate over the next few days."

Katie thrust another sheaf of paper in front of the Grand Dame. "If you'll just sign each sheet I'll implement the changes immediately."

"Just leave them there for me to review," Ms Lawton said wearily. All she could think of was how nice it would be to have a drink. A long, tall gin and tonic, with plenty of ice and a slice.

17

A Disagreeable Start to the Day

Ms Lawton reviewed the two punishment reports gloomily.

"You knew that Morton had been chucked out of assembly and had just received a mandatory bare bender, didn't you?" she asked.

Ms Whitton grinned. "Oh yes," she said smugly. "But you told me to beat her whenever the opportunity arose and she was late for orchestra practice so I gave her a damn good thrashing."

The Grand Dame sighed. Theoretically the Music Dame was correct. When she had first initiated the harsh regime of Operation Scorched Arse she had specifically instructed the Dames to treat Deborah Morton with extreme prejudice. Nonetheless, as she looked over the two reports again she couldn't help feeling that Ms Whitton had taken the definition of extreme prejudice to the limit.

"Morton, Phase 5, step up for goofing," screeched Janet Mitchell, waving her red card in the air.

Operation Scorched Arse

Deborah rolled her eyes and groaned. She slowly stood up and struggled passed her seated chums. At the end of the row of seats Mitch the Bitch was positively glowing with delight.

"Gotcha," she gloated as Deborah approached. "And by the way, your tie's undone," she cackled.

Deborah groaned again.

Deborah ran her tongue over her lips. She had been standing in disgrace at the front of the hall for almost ten minutes. She had done her best to look nonchalant but from the way she kept pursing her lips and drumming her fingers against the sides of her legs it was clear that she was nervous and agitated.

Debs' heart began to pound uncomfortably as she heard the click-clack of heels in the corridor outside the hall. Momentarily the doors swung open and the first members of the Brass entered.

The first wave barely paid her any heed, although several of the liberals, including Dotty Hammell, Pauline Gascoigne, Stephanie Powell and Jane Lummell threw her sympathetic smiles. The last of the Brass to enter were the Wart and Patty Hodge. They strode purposefully towards her.

"Oh you're going to make Ms Lawton's day," gloated the Wart. "I hope she thrashes you so hard you can't sit down for a week."

Deborah did her best not to flinch.

Patty grinned wolfishly and reached into her jacket pocket. She produced a red card and waved it in the air.

"Morton, Phase 5, red card for zero-tolerance collar and tie abuse," she announced gleefully. "Make an appointment with Miss Beck for a mandatory slippering."

Deborah felt her cheeks turn red.

Deborah Morton was sweating. The past twenty minutes had been most disagreeable. When Ms Lawton had arrived in the assembly hall she was plainly displeased to encounter Deborah and had made her feelings quite clear. She had verbally trashed Debs for several minutes before dismissing her with the ominous warning that she intended to beat her very, very soundly.

Katie Beck had been delighted to see Deborah. The unfortunate state of Debs collar and tie gave the unit's matron the opportunity to subject her to a comprehensive clobber inspection.

Deborah was notoriously clobber challenged and was consistently ranked amongst the five worst dressed inmates at the facility.

Katie took her time. Deborah stood with her hands on her head as the matron inspected every stitch of her clobber. Katie was a true artiste when it came to inspection. She started at the front, working her way down every individual button, looking for chips, loose threads or signs of premature discoloration. She checked every seam of Deborah's blouse and skirt. All the while she gave Debs a colorful commentary regarding the rump roasting she planned to give her the following morning.

Moving to the rear Katie was even more spiteful. She tut-tutted as she ran her fingers over more seams and muttered, "well, well and what have we here?" It was most disconcerting.

Operation Scorched Arse

Bottom inspection was no better. Katie left Debs sprawled bare arsed across the desk in the ante-room for a full five minutes before she came in to prod and pinch her backside.

Finally Deborah was left to stand on the landing, her hands on her head and her nose pressed to the wall while she waited anxiously for the arrival of the Grand Dame. Deborah Morton couldn't think of a more disagreeable way to start the day.

A Ration of Tongue Pie

Deborah Morton was sweating. Ms Lawton was an extremely articulate woman by nature and was at her most expressive when it came to the subject of malfeasance. Unfortunately for Deborah her lengthy history of mega-minxdom gave the Grand Dame copious scope to wax eloquent. Forced to stand to stiff attention, eyes front and still as a statue Deborah had no alternative but to chow down on an unappetizing ration of tongue pie.

Deborah unfastened the top button of her red and black striped blazer and shrugged it off. She felt totally drained. She felt as if she had been mauled by a mountain lion. The eloquent condemnation of her general misbehavior had seemed interminable and Deborah was almost relieved when Ms Lawton finally stepped out from behind her desk and crossed the room to the tall-boy that housed her collection of canes. But the Grand Dame hadn't quite finished. Deborah groaned inwardly as she was unexpectedly sucker-punched.

Operation Scorched Arse

"And one more thing, Morton," announced Ms Lawton as she selected a long thin cane and swished it through the air. "I'm about sick of your persistent collar and tie abuse. I'm going to instruct Katie to give you a double slippering in the morning. Now remove your blazer and bend over the chair."

Deborah thrust her hands into the pockets of her blazer as she tottered out of the Grand Dames study. There was no question that Ms Lawton had made good on her promise and beaten Deborah very, very soundly. Debs felt as if smoke was billowing out from underneath her skirt. Over the years Deborah's rear end had become a well-calibrated whopometer but she didn't need to inspect any gauges to know that she had just been totally nailed.

Ms Lawton took several deep breaths. Deborah was folded over the straight-backed chair in front of the fireplace. The skirt of her skirt and the tail of her blouse were meticulously folded back. Her navy blue gossamer bumbags were concertinaed around her ankles.
The Grand Dame took a tight grip on the thirty-six inch long cane and tapped it downwards.

Ms Lawton prided herself on her even-handedness. She came from the school of hard-whops and knew from bitter experience what it was like to be personally targeted. During the first four years of Deborah's sentence she had been sympathetic towards her celebrity inmate. She had suspected that Deborah's spectacular arrest and subsequent trashing in the press had been government vehicles to distract attention from yet another economic folly.

She had admired Deborah's intellect, musical prowess and sporting brilliance. Despite Deborah's natural tendency towards naughtiness the Grand Dame had indulged her and treated her as the golden gal. However, all that had changed in one trivial moment of collar and tie abuse and the events that succeeded it. No matter how hard she tried the Grand Dame was forced to concede that Deborah Morton had made a dizzying descent to the role of her personal bête noire.

She raised her arm slightly higher than normal and whipped the rattan rod through the air.

Deborah was having considerable difficulty putting it up and keeping it up. Ms Lawton always caned hard but this morning she was really putting her arm into it and every full-bloodied swipe made Debs teeth-chatter and her nerve-endings jangle. It took all her grit and determination to keep from howling.

Despite their differences Ms Lawton had considerable respect for Deborah's ability to take a licking with the minimum of fuss. She waited patiently between strokes, confident that Deborah would eventually settle back into the required position for the thrashing to proceed. Nonetheless, she could tell from the protracted wiggling and jiggling of Deborah's buttocks and the heartfelt pants she could hear her victim emitting that she had thoroughly nailed Debs Morton.

Operation Scorched Arse

Debs wriggled through the corridors, her arse on fire. It was Saturday morning and she needed to go to her study and pick up her clarinet for orchestra practice.

She crossed the quadrangle and making sure that there were no prefects lurking about she slipped behind the accommodation wing and sought out Rosemary's cigarette stash pile. Debs didn't really smoke, just one or two a week when she was feeling stressed and with her bum blazing like a furnace she was feeling particularly stressed.

She sucked down on the fag and looked down at her watch. The visit with Ms Lawton had been so protracted that she had missed almost half the practice. Nonetheless she wasn't too concerned. The piece that Ms Whitton had chosen for the recital was familiar and the last two rehearsals had gone swimmingly. She stubbed out her fag and flicked it into a nearby compost heap.

She headed back to the front door of the accommodation wing to fetch her clarinet and wished that her arse didn't burn so ferociously.

Extreme Prejudice

"I'm sorry I'm late Ma'am," Deborah muttered and hurried towards the empty seat amongst the orchestra.

"Where do you think you're going?" snapped Ms Whitton.

"To take my place Ma'am," responded Debs.

"Oh no you don't young lady, you will repair to the music room and bring me the Morton Special" said the Music Dame.

Deborah gaped at the instructor incredulously. "Whadaya mean?" she spluttered.

"You're late," said Ms Whitton imperiously. "Mandatory six of the best."

Debs continued to gape. "But you know why I'm late," she gasped. "I was in the Grand Dame's study."

"That's no excuse, this whole rehearsal has been a fiasco due to your selfish behavior," retorted Ms Whitton, "now do as you're told and bring me my bow."

Operation Scorched Arse

"This is ridiculous," Debs snapped back. "You're not going to beat me for this."

"Are you refusing to obey me?" asked Ms Whitton.

"You're damn right I am," said Debs obstinately.

"Very well Morton, I shall send someone else to fetch the bow and in the meantime I shall summons Jacqueline Ivanhoe and Yvonne Godfrey and I will have you held down."

The tension in the Great Hall was palpable.

"You rotten fucking bitch," Debs blurted out. "This is so fucking bogus."

"I'll count to five Miss Morton, it's your choice."

Deborah trudged through the corridors carrying the wooden violin bow that Ms Whitton had commissioned for the sole purpose of beating her. Her mind was racing; the heat in her backside was showing no signs of diminishing. The prospect of being thrashed with the customized rod was unthinkable.

Deborah desperately fought back her tears. The pain was excruciating. She was sprawled out across a low lying piano stool, her arms and legs stretched out into a full drape, her head well down and her arse well up. She sensed the Music Dame stepping in for the final swipe and squeezed her eyes tight.

Ms Whitton was a burly cove and was notorious for the venom with which she wielded the violin bow. When she commissioned the particular bow that she was wielding from a purveyor in

Southern Brazil she had specified an unusual stiffness for the shaft, explaining that it was for display purposes only. It was a truly lethal weapon.

Deborah's whole body reacted uncontrollably. Her legs kicked back, her hands gripped her head and she writhed so much that she almost rolled off the stool. It was a tremendous strike. The echo of wood rebounding off tautened gossamer reverberated around the far corners of the hall.

Debs looked ashen as she handed over her personal punishment record book for post-processing. The collar and tie that she had restored to a non-abusive condition was now skew-whiff. Her hair looked unkempt and the light trace of mascara she was allowed to wear was smudged across her face.

Wordlessly Ms Whitton annotated the book and then without warning she pointed back at the stool. "Now bend over again," she said curtly.

Debs mouth opened and her chin wagged but no sounds came out.

"You cussed me out," snapped Ms Whitton, "now bend over or I shall have you collared and taken up to the Grand Dames and demand you are given a public flogging."

Deborah Morton gaped at the music instructor. For a moment she said nothing and remained glued to the spot. Then finally she glared defiantly at Ms Whitton. "You'll never make me howl and you'll never make me blub," she said rebelliously and then hopelessly she leaned down and stretched her body out across the stool.

Operation Scorched Arse

Ms Lawton removed the cap of her pen and wearily signed her name at the bottom of the two punishment reports. Ms Whitton was looking positively smug as she strutted out of the door. The Grand Dame sighed and put her head in her hands.

"Extreme prejudice," chortled Ms Whitton in the saloon bar of the Bunch of Grapes. "I redefined extreme. Morton won't be sitting down comfortably for a month."

"Good work," saluted Patty Hodge. She raised her glass in the air. "To Operation Scorched Arse and may it never end."

Katie Beck, the Wart and Ms Whitton chinked glasses and winked conspiratorially.

Extreme Malice

Susan Lawton sipped a gin and tonic and considered her position. She would celebrate her fiftieth birthday during the next summer furlough although she took good care of herself and she looked ten years younger. She had been married once, to a military intelligence officer who had been gunned down while on a security detail in Central America. She had dated occasionally but never found anybody to her taste.

She was not without means. She would qualify for two military pensions. During her thirty plus years of public service she had pre-dominantly lived on expense accounts and had saved the bulk of her salary. When her parents had passed on she had inherited a substantial home, free of the burden of mortgage, and a healthy portfolio of stocks, shares and bearer bonds.

For the most part the Grand Dame believed that her ten-year tenure at the helm of the Woody Back to School unit had been a comprehensive

Operation Scorched Arse

success. She believed she had far exceeded the expectations of the Ministry of Extreme Social Rehabilitation when they had first opened the facility. Over a hundred of the nations most notorious Ladettes had been successfully rehabilitated into society, either finding worthwhile employment or entering universities as mature students.

She studied the two punishment reports and the 'Eyes Only' memorandum she had issued, declaring Deborah as the unit's Public Enemy Number One. She had intended to make life tough for Debs; to make an example of her for her belligerent behavior and her thoughtless attempt at revenge for being spanked. It had seemed a perfectly reasonable response. However, she had strongly emphasized to the Brass and the Elite that whilst Deborah was the subject of Hostile Targeting all beatings must be one hundred per cent legitimate.

Ms Whitton had been thorough. The reports were flawless; each cited the articles of the rules and regulations that justified the beatings. They also included a damning reference from her own memorandum that stated that, 'Morton should be treated with Extreme Prejudice at all times. All rules, regulations and protocols are to be strictly enforced. Infractions however minor should be treated with zero-tolerance and she should be punished to the maximum allowable extent.'

Ms Lawton couldn't deny that Ms Whitton had followed her instructions to the letter, although she suspected that the Music Dame had acted out of extreme malice rather than extreme prejudice. The first beating would have been controversial under any circumstances, but the second bordered on abuse of privilege.

The Grand Dame refreshed her glass. She felt weary. For ten years she had struggled to maintain the fine balance between the strict disciplinary requirements of the Extreme Social Rehabilitation program and the judicious use of discipline.

It had never been easy. Out of necessity she had recruited some of the nation's most notorious disciplinarians to impose the harsh requirement of the Social Rehabilitation program.

The Grand Dame was not naïve. She was fully aware that Patty had surrounded herself with supporters and had been preaching the virtues of a zero-tolerance policy long before Susan had imposed Operation Scorched Arse.

She had always carefully monitored Patty's activities. She knew from bitter and painful personnel experience that Patty was capable of embarking on a campaign of tyranny given half an opportunity

Susan sighed and stared down at the punishment reports lying on the table before her. She was wracked with guilt. What had started as a well-intentioned campaign to restore a semblance of order amongst the community had misguidedly supplied Patty and her cohorts with an ideal opportunity to embark upon a wave of tyranny.

She was beginning to acknowledge that Operation Scorched Arse may have been a tragic and unforgivable mistake.

Perhaps it was time to move on, she wondered to herself. She poured herself another stiff drink and

Operation Scorched Arse

was about to return to her seat when there was a knock on the door.

"I'm here to be caned," Cathryn Cassidy informed her in an indifferent drawl.

Miss Cathryn Cassidy

Cathryn was dressed in her prefect's garb of block red blazer with black piping around the border, white blouse, red tie and a dark pleated skirt. She wore a boater on her head at a jaunty angle.

"What is it this time Cassidy?" asked Ms Lawton.

"Curfew violation apparently," drawled Cat with a nonchalant shrug. "Patty says I didn't fill out some new fangled paperwork so she sent me up for whops."

"That is Ms Hodge to you, Cassidy," said the Grand Dame.

"Oh yeah, well whatever," said Cat indifferently.

Ms Lawton twitched her nose suspiciously. "Have you been drinking, Cassidy?" she asked.

"Naw, well yeah, but not drinking exactly, I had a couple of glasses of white wine, nothing serious. What are you going to do? Flog me?" said Cat in the same unconcerned drawl.

Operation Scorched Arse

"I will certainly be considering that option," snapped the Grand Dame.

Cathryn rolled her eyes.

Ms Lawton scowled at the prefect. "Raise your skirt," she said curtly.

"Oh good grief," said Cat. She reached under her skirt and extracted a packet of Marlboro Lights from the elastic waistband of her bumbags. "Are these what you're looking for?" she asked and tossed them on the desk.

"Your attitude is not helping you," said Ms Lawton. "You still have the remainder of the year before you complete the program and I can still flunk you. You know that alcohol and cigarettes are forbidden but you continue to flaunt the rules."

"Look Ma'am," said Cat. "I'm a prefect; I was out in town on a legitimate pass. I had a couple of scoops and I would have stashed the fags when I got back. If Patty, oops, Ms Hodge, hadn't introduced some new and unannounced protocol then nobody would be any the wiser."

Ms Lawton sighed. She always found dealing with Cathryn most disconcerting. During her years in Military Intelligence she had been trained to interrogate terrorists and enemies of the state. She was considered a master practitioner of the craft. However, in the nearly seven years that she had been responsible for overseeing Cathryn's social rehabilitation she had never managed to satisfactorily penetrate Cat's inner psyche.

It was not that Cathryn was devious or disingenuous. In fact quite the opposite, she was startling forthright and straight-forward. She wasn't rude or arrogant or even willfully disobedient. She merely seemed to have a total disregard for rules or convention and seemed quite content to suffer any consequences that might arise.

The Grand Dame wasn't naïve. She was aware that the inmates had stashes of booze and cigarettes secreted all over the facility. She occasionally instituted searches but the grounds were simply too large to police adequately. She had nothing in principle against drinking or smoking but had found in the early years of the unit's history a policy of moderation was impossible to enforce so she had implemented a total prohibition.

Ms Lawton looked over at Cathryn. In many ways the prefect was at the very heart of her problem. It was Cat after all who had authored the subversive manifesto of mega-minxdom and had rallied the inmates into the irksome cult. Nonetheless, the Grand Dame had considerable respect for Cathryn. She had got her hands on a bootleg copy of the doctrine and had been impressed by its witty and sophisticated articulation. She was also aware of Patty's deep dislike for Cat.

"What new fangled paperwork?" asked Ms Lawton.

Cathryn shrugged. "I dunno," she drawled. "I handed in my pass when I came back to the facility and then I got a summons. Patty, oh shit, Ms Hodge, told me that my paperwork was invalid and sent me over to see you, so here I am."

Ms Lawton leaned back in her chair thoughtfully. "Alright Cassidy," she said finally,

"Please step out onto the landing and assume the position. I'd like to look into this a little further."

Ms Lawton studied the two forms. "I must confess, I'm not sure I see the difference, Patricia," she told her deputy. "I mean they are laid out a little differently but they seem to contain the same information."

Patty narrowed her eyes. "As a member of the Elite Cassidy is supposed to keep abreast of all of the rules, regulations and protocols," she snapped. "If she was doing her job properly she would know which form is currently in use. This is a typical example of her irresponsible attitude to her responsibilities as a prefect."

"But Ms Hammell signed the town pass," observed the Grand Dame. "That at least lends it some legitimacy."

"Dotty Hammell is a damned liberal," snorted Patty.

"Alright Patty leave it with me and send Cassidy in on your way out," sighed Susan Lawton.

An Epic Scolding

"She's losing her nerve," scoffed Patty in the saloon Bar of the Bunch of Grapes. "She let that degenerate Cassidy off Scot-free. It's a disgrace."

Patty had assembled her cohorts for a Council of War.

Katie snorted contemptuously. "She rejected several of my amendments to the Politics of Clobber," she complained.

"Do you think she's reconsidering Operation Scorched Arse?" wailed the Wart.

Patty shook her head firmly. "She's too invested now. If she shows the slightest sign of weakness pandemonium will ensue. She'll never let that happen."

Susan Lawton slid into bed. Her decision to release Cathryn without punishment had helped to assuage her feeling of guilt. Nonetheless she still had difficulty sleeping and eventually resorted to pouring herself a stiff brandy. She closed her eyes and did her best to put the complexities of Operation Scorched

Operation Scorched Arse

Arse out of her mind as she drifted into the land of nod.

Any inclinations Ms Lawton may have harbored of moving towards a position of détente were immediately dispelled when she entered the assembly hall on Monday morning and found Deborah Morton standing in the familiar pose of disgrace for the second time in the space of three days.

Deborah's chums were transfixed as they watched the drama unfold. When the Grand Dame first observed Deborah her expression changed momentarily to one of open-mouthed incredulity. As she took the ten steps between the doors of the hall and the spot where Deborah was waiting her features quickly rearranged themselves into undisguised vexation.

Deborah was visibly anxious. Her mouth twitched and her eyes darted nervously as the Grand Dame approached. At first Ms Lawton seemed at a loss for words. She fixed Deborah with a gimlet gaze. Debs gamely tried to return the Grand Dames stare.

There was a brief and ominous silence in the hall as the two women stared at each other, but it was just a lull before the storm.

It did not take long for Ms Lawton to find her voice. She leaned her face in close to Deborah and unleashed her tongue. Every inmate in the hall had experienced a scolding from Ms Lawton at one time or another but thankfully they were generally delivered in the privacy of her study.

The Grand Dame didn't raise her voice, choosing instead to use a tone so icy that it sent shivers down the spines of the watching inmates. Deborah recoiled under the verbal assault.

It was a scolding on an epic scale. It was the general consensus amongst the inmates that the Grand Dame stayed up late at nights poring over ancient tomes and lexicons searching for new variations of the word malfeasance. She seemed intent on demonstrating the full extent of her vocabulary as she publicly denounced Deborah.

Debs did her best not to flinch under the scathing attack but she could feel her cheeks turning bright red and she was having increasing difficulty meeting the Grand Dames eye.

Deborah trudged out of the hall. This mornings public scolding had made the one she had received two days earlier seem like a cozy chat over tea and crumpets. She felt mentally and physically drained as she dispiritedly made her way through the corridors.

The past forty-eight hours had not been kind to Deborah Morton's rear end. Her nailing by the Grand Dame and the heinous double beating by Ms Whitton had been excruciating. The following morning she had been forced to pitch up at Katie's to be slippered for collar and tie abuse. The unit matron had taken great relish in putting Debs over her knee and had spanked her so hard it had brought tears to Deborah's eyes.

Deborah had been forced to spend most of the weekend standing up. As she cut through the corridors it occurred to Debs that if the Grand Dame decided to lay it on as thick as she had on Saturday morning she was in for a very disagreeable experience. Deborah Morton was not faint of heart

Operation Scorched Arse

but the thought of the impending six of the best sent a shiver up her spine.

Katie was delighted to see Deborah. She sensed that Debs was not her usual cocksure self and added to her misery with some disparaging remarks of her own.

When she sent Deborah into the ante-room to bend over the desk she left Debs butt-naked for a full ten minutes before going into inspect her.

Deborah pressed her nose against the wall and placed her hands on top of her head. Her heart pounded uncomfortably under her crisp white blouse and she felt a line of perspiration forming on her brow as she waited to be caned.

A Poor Beleaguered Bum

Standing gloomily on the landing with Katie watching her like a hawk Debs had little else to do but ruminate on her latest disaster.

It had been a classic Debs moment. One moment she was sitting calmly in the assembly hall waiting for the arrival of the Brass, the next moment she inexplicably reached her leg out and slid the satchel of the gal seated in front of her along the floor and out of reach, forcing her to scramble to retrieve it. It was a totally mindless action that wasn't even particularly funny and was totally lacking in guile.

Nonetheless Deborah felt a momentary jag of exhilaration, a strange and satisfying buzz. It was short-lived. Almost immediately she came back to her senses with a crash. Anxiously she had turned her head and looked towards the end of the row of seats. She watched as Janet Mitchell theatrically reached into the pocket of her blazer and extracted her red-card.

Operation Scorched Arse

Deborah had no explanation for her action. She had not planned it and had not even been aware that she was doing it until it was too late. It was a problem that had plagued her for a decade and a half and had been the primary reason why she seemed to permanently wear red stripes across her bum. However, Debs doubted that Ms Lawton would be sympathetic to the explanation that she wasn't really responsible for her actions and that she had been momentarily overwhelmed by an inner devil that took control.

Deborah's assessment of Ms Lawton's sympathy level was proving unerringly correct. In the Grand Dame's opinion Deborah's ridiculous prank was just another example of her lack of self-control. Wisely Debs elected not to introduce the notion of other-worldly influences into the proceedings. The Grand Dame was clearly not in the mood for listening.

Much to Deborah's dismay Ms Lawton was in the mood for spanking. The Grand Dame had ordered her to remove her blazer then taken her by the wrist and led her across to a convenient chair.

Head down and arse up over Ms Lawton's knee Deborah Morton was beginning to sweat. The hand-spanking of an inmate as advanced in her social rehabilitation program as Deborah was extremely rare. Generally they were limited to acting as precursors to public floggings. However, Deborah got the impression that this was a purely private matter and Ms Lawton's way of reinforcing to Deborah that she was firmly ensconced as number one on her shit-list.

Ms Lawton was using a blitz and wait tactic. She had Deborah tucked tightly into the crease of her lap, bent like a bow with her head well down and her arse well up. Periodically the Grand Dame would deliver a barrage of hearty spanks and then leave an uncomfortably long time to allow the results to sink in thoroughly.

Debs hung upside down panting. Ms Lawton was a slender elegant woman but the palm of her right hand was unexpectedly potent. The flesh of Deborah's backside was soon painted a vivid crimson as the Grand Dame worked up one side and back down the other.

The intermissions were most disconcerting. Debs had no idea when the next bevy of spanks would arrive. Bent so far over she was helpless to look back, her nose was only inches from the Brazilian redwood floor of the Grand Dame's study. She was completely at Ms Lawton's mercy.

Deborah looked nervously at the long thin cane that Ms Lawton was flexing between her hands. The prospect of the whippy rattan rod lashing across her well spanked rear end would have been unappealing at any time but the Grand Dame had just delivered some devastating news.

"Your behavior this term has been deplorable," Ms Lawton had informed her. "On Saturday morning I gave you six of the very best and I assumed that would be enough to deter you from continuing on this foolish bout of reckless behavior. Clearly it had no effect whatsoever."

Operation Scorched Arse

Deborah looked at the Grand Dame bleakly. She did not like the direction that this conversation was going.

"I am determined to rehabilitate you successfully and am willing to take whatever measures that requires," continued Ms Lawton, "now go and bend over the chair. I intend to give you twelve strokes and that will remain your punishment on any future visits to this office until you can satisfactorily demonstrate that there is a marked and consistent improvement in your behavior."

Deborah continued to stare at the Grand Dame bleakly. She wondered whether it was an appropriate time to introduce her little devil theory into the proceedings.

The Woody Mantra

Deborah Morton plucked up her courage and bent forward at the waist. She placed her hands on the front edge of the seat of the straight backed chair and then reached down and gripped the crossbar, one hand at a time. She was feeling quite bilious.

"I would strongly suggest that you spend the Christmas furlough reconsidering your behavior," the Grand Dame had informed her as she extracted a long thin cane from the tallboy. "There are not many nails left to bang into your coffin. Now go over there and bend over the chair."

Deborah just groaned.

Twelve strokes of the cane delivered across a well-spanked bottom is nothing to be sniffed at. Debs prided herself that no matter how difficult circumstances became in her rear end that she would never howl and never blub. Bent over the chair with her scarlet backside totally defenseless she reckoned she was faced with a daunting task.

Operation Scorched Arse

Ms Lawton swung the cane with lethal precision. Despite her state of extreme irritation the Grand Dame was a consummately professional martinet. As a graduate from the school of hard whops Susan Lawton understood the intricate mechanics of a high-performance licking. Every stroke was delivered cleanly across the sweet spot of Deborah's backside in a tight formation. Ms Lawton was determined that Deborah would suffer nothing worse than a very hot bottom.

Debs gritted her teeth. Each explosive swipe of the thirty-six inch senior cane was excruciating, but she was in the zone. "It's only whops," she repeated over and over in her head. The popular Woody mantra helped her to stay focused and not howl or blub or make a muff of herself.

The 'its only whops' mantra originated with Deborah's best chum Rosemary Booker. Rosemary had entered the Woody Back to School unit sporting a virgin arse; she had never been spanked in her life, let alone caned. However, following her introduction to being whapped with a whippy stick her reaction became a Woody legend.
"I can't see what all the fuss is about," she told her chums. "After all it was only whops."

Debs knew the form. After each stroke she wriggled and jiggled her body in agitation as the impact of the wicked stick traversed her central nervous system. Despite her discomfort she would regroup and slowly reposition her upturned derriere for the next nerve jangling, teeth chattering strike.

Debs tottered out of the study like a drunken sailor on shore leave. She kept her fists balled in her blazer pockets to avoid the temptation of rubbing.

According to the protocols she was required to proceed directly to the lecture room but she decided to risk making a brief detour to a nearby bathroom.

She stared at herself in the mirror. She looked disheveled. During spanking the knot of her tie had slipped down and her blouse looked crumpled. Her face was ashen and her hair needed brushing.

She reached under her skirt and very gently rolled down her bumbags. She winced as she peeled the material off the throbbing weals. She raised her skirt and inspected her backside in the mirror. It was a mess. Ms Lawton had been extremely thorough. She had not missed a centimeter of Deborah's bum during the spanking and the flesh was still pulsating. The center of her buttocks were covered with thin red stripes in a very tight formation. The last stroke had cut across the existing stripes. She winced as she ran her fingers along the weals.

She found a paper towel and doused it with cold water. She pressed it against her poor beleaguered bum. After a few minutes she dried herself off and replaced her bumbags.

She washed her face and brushed her hair. She straightened her tie and picked up her satchel. With considerable lack of enthusiasm at the prospect of having to plonk her wounded arse on a hard wooden chair seat she wriggled off towards the lecture rooms.

At every opportunity Deborah's chums rallied around to comfort and console her. Debs' recent trials

Operation Scorched Arse

and tribulations had been the hot topic on the gossvine. They praised her for her courage and fortitude and assured her that nothing would divert them from the campaign of mischief and mayhem. Debs did her best to be gracious; it was the camaraderie of the inmates that made incarceration at the nations most austere Back to School unit bearable. Nonetheless, Deborah Morton just wished that her arse didn't throb so badly.

"Come on, Debs," Rosemary said cheerfully. "It was only whops," as she spread Deborah out across her lap and began to rub one of her mystical balms into the steamy weals.

"Yeah, rock on Rosie," groaned Debs, "you know what sister? Sometimes I think that you're fucking barking!"

"Woof! Woof!" giggled Rosie and continued to massage the soothing aloe-based creams into the swollen stripes.

"We're back full steam ahead," gloated Patty. "I told you that there was nothing to fret about. She signed off all the amendments to the protocols including the Politics of Clobber stuff that she rejected before."

Katie, the Wart and Ms Whitton beamed gleefully and chugged back tequila slammers. Patty ordered a bottle of bubbles and put it on Katie's tab.

"Bottoms up," she toasted, "here's to Operation Scorched Arse."

25

Jojo

Deborah wasn't the only one experiencing hot and sweaty times. In fact despite her recent spate of bottom poundings Debs was not even ranked as the terms number one on the Hall of Shame. As usual that honor fell to the unit's most incorrigible mega-minx, Joanna Heyworth. Jojo was beautiful, vivacious and very, very naughty. Jojo japed and larked and pranked and rubbished the pre's relentlessly. She was fearless and her fellow inmates considered her to be the embodiment of the spirit of mega-minxdom.

Jojo was standing outside the door of the library with her hands on her head. She was waiting to be dangled.
In some ways Joanna was an unlikely candidate to hold the rank of All-Time Big BUTT. When she arrived at the facility she was sporting a virgin arse. Neither her parents nor the school she had attended had practiced corporal punishment. Nonetheless this state of affairs was soon rectified and she was the first of the new entrants to be

Operation Scorched Arse

spanked. Jojo took it in her stride and later she would become the first Little Brat in the unit's history to be caned.

Jojo had a natural flair for minxing. She found herself in good company. Along with her best chum Nicola Jane Nixon, Rosemary Booker and Debs were also starting their sentences. It was a magical time for minxes and a recipe for mischief and mayhem. Jojo and her chums quickly gained respect from the veteran mega-minxes and were dubbed the Famous Four.

The Big BUTT was hotting up and competition was fierce. Jojo threw her bumbags into the ring with wild abandon. Every year she established new records on the Hall of Shame including becoming the first inmate to score the elusive Bull when she was caned over fifty times during the fourth year of her sentence.

Operation Scorched Arse was proving predictably hot and sweaty for Joanna. Once the program had been announced she had defiantly declared that "I'm going to get whopped anyway, so I might as well get whopped for having fun."

Jojo's idea of fun and the prefect's idea of fun did not always coincide. The prefects and most particularly Yvonne Godfrey and her SS cohorts took considerable umbrage to being royally rubbished by the petite redhead. They brought her to the library and thrashed her frequently and they routinely added red marks on the card bearing her name on the card index system in the prefect's common room.

Penelope Ann Evans was changing out of her riding togs when her personal grubby, Jennifer Gardiner, stopped by.

"Jojo's outside the library waiting to be dangled," she informed the Red-shirt.

Penny Ann frowned. "Who gave you the envelope?" she asked.

"Mitchell, Ma'am," Jen told her.

Penny Ann continued to frown. She wasn't surprised. This was the fourth time she would be forced to dangle Jojo in the space of thirteen weeks. Invariably the critical fifth red mark was awarded by a member of the SS.

"Thank you, Jennifer, you can cut along now," Pen grunted.

Penelope Ann pulled her red-shirt off a hanger and shrugged it on, buttoning the front quickly. She had come to hate her job. Jojo and Pen had been chums years before they were sent to the Big House. They were both internationally famous equestrians and had ridden together on the national team. The prospect of having to dangle her chum again was very unappealing.

Earlier in the week Penny Ann had made another vain attempt to lodge an official complaint against the SS but as usual she was thwarted by Patty Hodge.

"I have reviewed every thrashing report tendered by the members of the Elite against whom you are making these scurrilous accusations," Patty had retorted imperiously, "and frankly I am reaching the end of my tether with you. I am considering filing an application to have you stood down and replaced

Operation Scorched Arse

by a more appropriate candidate such as Yvonne Godfrey."

Penny Ann had done her best to stand her ground but she was lambasted in a most disagreeable manner.

Penelope Ann had even tried to make a covert appointment with the Grand Dame but Katie Beck had stone-walled her. Within an hour she was summonsed back to the Deputy Grand Dame's study for another tongue lashing. It was not a good time to be a liberal Red-shirt.

The Fine Art of Dangling

Jojo followed Penelope Ann into the library. She knew the form; she strode down the room to the far end. She peeled off her blazer and folded it neatly, and then went over and picked up the spanking stool and placed in front of the over-sized fireplace.

Behind her Penny Ann was removing her own blazer and rolling up the sleeves of her red blouse. She loosened her tie and unfastened her top button. She reached under her blouse and retrieved the key she wore around her neck. She crossed to a side table and unlocked a drawer. The Red-shirt extracted a long handled, oval-headed, wood-backed hairbrush.

Penelope Ann sat up on the tall spanking stool with Jojo standing to her right hand side. Once Pen was in position Joanna offered her wrist so that she could be helped over and up.

When Katie Beck had first spotted the tall stool in a local antique store she had been immediately impressed with its possibilities. The stool was taller

Operation Scorched Arse

than a normal bar-stool and the crossbars were designed diagonally beneath the seat.

Katie was already celebrating her latest success. She had recently persuaded Ms Lawton to allow her to replace the traditional ashplant wielded by the Red-shirt's with the more lethally punishing hairbrush. The transition was not popular amongst the inmates; particularly as they were forced to spread-eagle themselves across Katie's lap while they were being spanked. Her eyes lit up when she saw the stool and she immediately got out her cheque-book.

"I was fucking dangling," Claire Brooks had complained to her chums after the official inauguration of the spanking stool into Woodyworld. "I couldn't touch the ground on either side and I had nothing to hold onto."

Penelope Ann neatly folded back Joanna's skirt and the tail of her blouse before rolling down her bumbags. She looped her left arm around Jojo's waist and made sure she was tucked in firmly. The Red-shirt slowly circled the wooden oval head of the hairbrush across the naked flesh of Joanna's right buttock.

"I'm going to need you to put it up and keep it up," she said.

Jojo just grunted.

Penelope Ann Evans raised the brush about eighteen inches above Jojo's defenseless flesh and brought it down with a loud crack.

A truly fine dangling needs to be delivered long, slow and juicy. Despite her distaste at having to punish Jojo Penny Ann had her reputation to consider. Every year the Red-shirt's vied for gaining the status of being the hottest spanker ever. Pen was already getting rave reviews from the whop-hardened mega-minxes and had no intention of letting the small matter of friendship get in her way.

Jojo didn't expect any slack. She fully understood that Penelope Ann was merely doing her duty. She settled in and focused on getting into the zone. The first time Penny Ann had dangled her Jojo had been at a disadvantage. Unbeknownst to Joanna Ms Lawton had amended the protocols and decreed that inmates in Phase 5, or above, of their sentences would be subjected to a full twelve spanks of the brush. Jojo had been caught by surprise when a seventh spank had arrived and had been nailed for the first time in her illustrious career. She had no intention of that happening again.

Penny Ann was being thorough. She slowly worked up one side of Jojo's bum and back down the other. The oval headed brush that Katie Beck had selected was perfectly designed to redden every square centimeter of the sweet spot in six easy spanks. The Woody connoisseurs were of a collective mind that this level of bum burning was quite ample and that an additional six spanks was completely unnecessary in furthering their goals of social rehabilitation.

Operation Scorched Arse

A perfectly timed twelve stroke dangling takes precisely three minutes to execute. This may not sound like a long time but for the victim dangled head down, arse up, with their arms and legs flapping helplessly it seems like eternity. Even for a veteran like Jojo the experience was quite taxing. By the time she wriggled out of the library Joanna Heyworth was feeling decidedly whop-weary.

Ivan Takes a Tumble

On the day before the unit closed down for the Christmas furlough Lady Victoria Brompton was caned in front of the assembled inmates.

Dressed in a crisp white blouse, striped tie and skin-tight whopping bags Victoria strode towards the vaulting horse and fearlessly bent over. The inmates watched her with considerable admiration.

Ms Lawton looked from the disheveled prefect to the defiant looking aristocrat.

Jackie Ivanhoe's left eye was showing signs of swelling and she was patting her nose with a handkerchief.

"She busted my dose," spluttered Ivan the Terrible tearfully.

Victoria curled her lip contemptuously. "Your nose ain't busted," she said scornfully, "if I'd wanted to bust it I would have."

The Grand Dame's study was crowded with members of the SS baying for blood.

Operation Scorched Arse

"She assaulted Ivan," bayed Yvonne. "It was completely unprovoked."

"She's a violent thug," squealed Mitch the Bitch.

"She needs to be sacked and put in chokey," insisted Spanker Spage.

"She's a menace to society," agreed Undies.

"Fawk off the lot of you," snarled Lady Vix, "before I punch all of your lights out."

"Time out," snapped Ms Lawton. "Now tell me what really happened and I don't want to hear any porkies."

Yvonne Godfrey approached Rachel Cox in the middle of the recreation area and showed her a red-card.

"Collar her and bring her to the library," she instructed Jackie Ivanhoe. "Six of the best for unruly behavior."

Rachel glared at Yvonne. "Don't be ridiculous, this is totally bogus."

Yvonne shrugged. "Take it up with your lawyer," she said off-handedly. "Collar her Ivan and let's go get us some whops."

Ivan the Terrible puffed herself up and made a grab for Rachel, intending to spin her around and secure her in an arm-lock. Rachel dodged out of the way.

"Get your hands off me you stupid bitch," she growled.

Ivan made a second equally unsuccessful attempt.

"Leave her alone," said Victoria in an assertive voice and stepped protectively in front of Rachel.

"Keep out of this Brompton," snapped Yvonne, "this is Elite business."

Ivan the Terrible pushed her face into Victoria's. "Yeah piss off Brompton before I box your ears," she hissed. Seconds later she landed unceremoniously on her substantial arse, holding her nose, clutching at her eye and howling like a muff.

Lady Victoria Brompton had been taught to box and wrestle by her four elder brothers on the grounds of the ancestral pile. She had a reputation as a pugnacious cove but many of the weaker inmates had reason to be grateful for the speed with which she was willing to put up her dukes. Lady Victoria Brompton could not tolerate bullying and over the years had regularly come to the rescue of inmates who were being roughed up by members of the Elite.

Ms Lawton did her best to disguise her secret amusement. Ivan the Terrible was still boohooing and demanding that Lady Victoria was sacked. Ms Lawton had some sympathy for Victoria's intervention on Rachel's behalf. She was well aware that being collared was an undignified and ignominious experience.

Nonetheless, bopping prefects on their sniffers was a serious offense and clearly Victoria needed to be punished very severely.

"Go next door and get yourself prepared for a flogging," she told Victoria.

"A flogging?" wailed Ivan. "You're letting her off with a wimpy old flogging? I want her charged with assault. She needs to go to chokey."

Operation Scorched Arse

Ms Lawton scowled at Jackie Ivanhoe. "While I cannot condone inmates taking the law into their own hands, I am aware that some of your collaring practices are barely legitimate. I shall be watching you closely in the future Miss Ivanhoe and if I get a whiff of a scent that you are abusing the collaring protocols you'll find out just how wimpy a flogging feels."

Jackie Ivanhoe pouted sourly.

28

I'll Be Watching You

Lady Victoria considered a public flogging to be a decent return on investment for the joy she had received from dumping Ivan on her arse. The look of amazement on the prefect's face when Victoria had unleashed a perfect rat-a-tat left-right combination had been priceless.

Victoria Brompton was no newcomer to being publicly flogged. In fact it was one of the few records she held over Jojo.

"It's only whops," she was fond of saying, "just whops in front of a few more people."

The inmates watched the proceedings with expert eyes. They were proud of Victoria and as far as they were concerned she was taking one for the team. Unusually Ms Lawton didn't seem to be laying it on too thick. She was swinging her arm at a leisurely pace and seemed to slow down at the last moment. They exchanged knowing glances. For some

Operation Scorched Arse

undisclosed reason the Grand Dame appeared to be cutting Her Ladyship some slack.

"You were pulling the strokes," complained Patty. "Brompton pops one of my prefects on the hooter and you cut her slack? What type of message do you think that sent to the other inmates?"

Ms Lawton narrowed her eyes. "Your prefects, Patricia?" she asked.

"You know what I mean," said Patty. "I manage the Elite."

"You manage the Elite on my behalf," said Ms Lawton pointedly. "Which brings me to the subject of Miss Godfrey."

It was Patty's turn to narrow her eyes. "Miss Godfrey? What about her?"

Yvonne looked uncomfortable. She did not like the tone of Ms Lawton's voice.

"What exactly was Cox doing that was so unruly?" asked the Grand Dame.

"She was causing a disturbance," muttered Yvonne.

"What kind of disturbance?" asked Ms Lawton pointedly.

"She was making a racket and a general nuisance of herself," said Yvonne defensively. "We all know from experience that behavior like that quickly escalates and the next thing we know we've got pandemonium on our hands."

"Did you show her a yellow card?"

"Well no. I decided that whops were the best course of action, so I requested Jackie Ivanhoe to collar her and take her to the library," explained Yvonne. "It was all done within the correct protocols."

"Where is Cox now?"

"She's outside the library," said Yvonne. "I was on my way to beat her when you summonsed me."

Ms Lawton pressed a button on her telephone.

"Katie, send a grubby to the library to tell Miss Cox that she's free to go," she said authoritatively.

Yvonne gaped at the Grand Dame. To the best of her knowledge Ms Lawton had never previously intervened and vetoed a prefectorial beating.

"Any questions?" asked the Grand Dame.

Yvonne Godfrey shook her head. "No, Ma'am'" she muttered.

"Good," said Ms Lawton, "and please remember, Miss Godfrey, that I'll be watching you."

"Bend over the desk," Patty instructed Yvonne Godfrey.

The prefect gaped at Patty. "Are you fucking kidding me? That's not funny."

Patty shrugged. "Just bend over; I need to make an example of you to distract the Grand Dame. She's sniffing about and not behaving rationally. We don't want her investigating SS business. You made a critical error of judgment and we need to make sure that she sees that you have been punished appropriately."

Yvonne stared at Patty. "A critical error of judgment? Rachel Cox was on your hit-list, I was following your instructions!" she squealed.

"Sometimes Yvonne you just have to take one for the team, now be a good gal and remove your blazer and bend over the desk," said Patty, flexing her

Operation Scorched Arse

long, thin wye-tipped cane between her hands. "Don't worry I'm only going to give you six."

"Oh my only Aunt Sally," was all that Yvonne Godfrey, commandant of the SS, could think of to say.

Sacrificial Bumbags

Yvonne Godfrey was hopping around her study, with her hands clutched to the seat of her skirt and was cussing up a storm to her cohorts.

"She beat me fucking bandy," bitched Yvonne. "She's deranged. She gave me specific instructions to target Rachel Cox and then she tells me I made a critical error of judgment."

Yvonne's lieutenants were appropriately sympathetic. For all her faults Yvonne Godfrey was certainly not a muff and could take a whopping with the best of them. However, from the frantic manner that she was publicly rubbing her arse they understood that she was experiencing some quite considerable gyp.

Even though she had promised Yvonne unlimited protection in her role as Commandant of the SS, Patty Hodge felt no compunction whatsoever about bending the prefect over her desk and thrashing her with a wye-tipped cane. As far as she was concerned it was a legitimate political maneuver to placate Ms Lawton.

Operation Scorched Arse

Patty sized up her target. She was not going to allow the small matter that they were supposed to be allies to get in the way of delivering a real sound licking. She placed her feet firmly and raised her arm in the air. With a terrific swipe she unleashed hell in Yvonne Godfrey's bumbags.

Yvonne was stretched out across Patty's large oak desk with her arms dangling over the far side. The wye-tip of the cane swiped down, the tip landing across the crown of her right buttock and etching her like a branding iron. The pain was excruciating. She felt quite bilious as the tremendous swipe burned deeper and deeper below her flesh. She clenched her teeth to stop from howling.

Patty was enjoying herself. She felt certain that the Grand Dame would approve of her decision to thrash Yvonne so she saw no reason not to enjoy herself. She took aim and swung her vicious cane with lethal force.

Patty worked over Yvonne's right buttock first, three deadly swipes, each landing inches apart, designed to create the maximum mischief and mayhem in Godders' bumbags.

Once she was finished with the right cheek, she laid down her cane and poured herself a gin and tonic.

"How am I doing?" she asked Yvonne.

"Grrrrrrrrrrrrrrrrrrr!" was all she got as a response.

Patty sipped her gin and tonic. She was in her comfort zone. She knew that Yvonne would bitch and moan about being beaten but she'd get over it.

Yvonne Godfrey was seething. Her right buttock was on fire and although she was not enthusiastic about a similar inferno being ignited in her left cheek the cavalier manner with which Patty was treating her was reprehensible.

Patty grinned to herself. Yvonne was beginning to show signs of considerable agitation. She was trying to look over her shoulder to work out what her controller was doing but it was impossible. Patty finished her drink, swiped up the cane, took aim and unleashed a perfect strike in one fluid motion. Yvonne Godfrey's legs scissored in consternation. Patty Hodge continued to grin.

"I'm sure that you'll be pleased that I took care of business," Patty told Ms Lawton. "I whole-heartedly agreed with you that Yvonne stepped over the line today and I felt it best to make an example of her."

Ms Lawton looked at Patty noncommittally. "It's Christmas, Patricia, and I think we all need a well-deserved break," she said. "Although we must remain committed to Operation Scorched Arse I'm hoping that the furlough will allow some of the recent unpleasantnesses to be forgotten and that we can start the new term in a slightly less hostile atmosphere."

"Absolutely, Susan," responded Patty unctuously. "I couldn't agree more. That's exactly why I deemed it necessary to make an example of

Godfrey. She'll spread the word amongst the zealots that we're not going to put up with anymore of their shenanigans."

Ms Lawton looked at Patty dubiously. It was her opinion that Patty Hodge had merely sacrificed Yvonne Godfrey's bumbags as a pacifier. She very much doubted that Patricia Hodge had any intention of reining in the Secret Sorority of Serial Spankers.

"We'll just have to wait and see," she said quietly.

Cool Arse Christmas

When the siren sounded to announce the official commencement of the three week Christmas furlough Debs Morton was packed and ready to go.

"What time is your Dad's chopper scheduled to arrive?" she demanded.

Nixdown Nixon just yawned and winked. "Shortly," she assured Debs.

Deborah paced up and down the study that Nix and Jojo shared.

"I want to get out of here," she grumbled. "Just think, three whole weeks with a cool arse."

The parking lot was filled with limos, taxis and the vehicles of friends and families of the inmates. There were several air-conditioned buses available to take gals to the train station. In the distance the highly anticipated helicopter approached to take Nix, Jojo, Debs and Rosemary to Nixdown's parent's beachside pad.

Operation Scorched Arse

Under the terms of their sentences the inmates were allowed three furloughs a year. Their activities were monitored by their Court Appointed Guardians and curfews were strictly imposed.

The inmates had learned that the best way to remain under the radar was to avoid the boisterous Ladette party scene that had caused them to be incarcerated in the first place and make their own fun.

Despite being banged up together twenty-four seven for thirty nine weeks of the year the inmates generally elected to spend the majority of the furloughs in each others company.

There was no shortage of private hideaways where they could kick back and have fun away from the prying eyes of the Dark Agents of the System.

Nixdown Nixon's father made his coastal villa with its private beach available to his daughter. It was a favorite hideaway for Nix and her chums.

Lord Brompton hosted open house at the castle and the Brompton New Years party was a must-attend event for the mega-minxes.

Christopher and Caroline Cassidy's Mayfair mansion was another popular haunt. Chris Cassidy hosted late-night jam sessions featuring his stable of stars from his successful jazz label.

As usual at intimate dinner parties whops and clobber was the most common subject of conversation. The inmates dissected the events of the past thirteen weeks. Undoubtedly the introduction of Operation Scorched Arse had heralded a new and painful era at the facility. The whop rate had escalated and the constant revisions to the rules, regulations and protocols had eliminated most of the minor freedoms and privileges that had existed previously. Consensus was that things would not improve in the foreseeable future.

"Here's to cool arse Christmas," was the common toast. "Let's enjoy it while we can."

Patty Hodge hosted a private party for her cronies on the Radical Right and the five members of the SS.

She complimented her guests on their performance during the past months but informed them that there 'was still much work to do.'

Patty had worked up detailed plans for even more extreme hostile targeting of the Dirty Dozen but warned her acolytes that, "we must be careful, we don't want any repetition of the mistakes you made at the end of the last term."

Yvonne Godfrey was still seething from the vicious thrashing she had received from Patty and demanded guarantees of protection of the SS's bumbags.

"I can't guarantee against your stupidity," Patty snapped back, "you made a dumb move and you paid the price. Now put on your big gal bumbags and get with the program."

Yvonne Godfrey muttered darkly.

Ms Lawton spent the Christmas furlough struggling with a crisis of conscience. She pored over the punishment statistics. Even when she took into account a small percentage of punishments that had resulted from over-zealous interpretations of hostile

Operation Scorched Arse

targeting and extreme prejudice the continuing rise of mega-minxdom was indisputable.

It was not just the whop rate of the Radical Right that had increased. Punishments by the liberals such as Dotty Hammell, Pauline Gascoigne, Stephanie Powell and Jane Lummell were also on the rise. Melanie White, who acted in the dual role of Deputy Headgal and Dorm Raider, and was an active and outspoken opponent of the SS, had caned more gals than any other prefect during a similar time-frame.

She spent time with her ward, Katie Beck. As usual Katie spent most of the time advocating new additions to the Politics of Clobber. Once when Ms Lawton had tired of the subject and asked Katie to drop it, her ward had continued. Wearily Ms Lawton put Katie over her knee and gave her a damn good spanking.

Susan Lawton began to plan her exit strategy.

Hot Arse Christmas

While the majority of the inmates were enjoying cool arse Christmas Claire Brooks was having no such luck.

Claire was the eldest daughter of pro-spanking activists Ma and Christopher Brooks. They were frequent guests on chat shows decrying the efforts of STOPP to eliminate the cane from the classroom.

Ma was regularly seen on TV showing off her hairbrush and preaching her mantra that 'there is no problem that can't be solved by a sore bottom.'

The Brooks hairbrush had been handed down through generations of Ma's side of the family. According to family lore the tradition originated with a Victorian Governess named Mary Whittington who operated a small private school specializing in correcting the willful or wayward ways of daughters of the British aristocracy. She found applying the back of a hairbrush to their noble backsides to be an extremely effective technique. She saw no reason why the techniques should not be deployed

Operation Scorched Arse

domestically on her own daughter's behinds and the tradition had begun. The hairbrush was handed from daughter to daughter as they were married and had families of their own.

Ma Brooks' mother had been an ardent disciplinarian and is credited with inventing the fine art of zinging. Ma was by all accounts a rebellious cove and according to Ma on one occasion she had not shown a satisfactory reaction to being spanked and the family matriarch had suddenly forced her head down and her bottom up and landed three mighty cracks, one on top of the other. Another family tradition had evolved.

Claire had elected to spend the majority of the furlough at her parent's house. She was well aware that if she was hoping for a cool arse Christmas this was a calculated gamble. It was a gamble that had back-fired in spades.

Many of Claire's problems resulted from her motor-mouth and her penchant for pith. Her habit of opening her mouth before engaging her brain had resulted in her persistently yanked out her seat in the lecture rooms and spread eagled across her desk. While her fellow inmates thought she was a hoot even the most enlightened members of the Brass found her infuriating.

Ma was not long on pith, especially when it involved potty-mouthing.

"You are an intelligent and articulate young woman," Ma was fond of telling Claire, "so you have no reason to resort to bar-room language."

Ma's lectures were generally conducted with her daughter head down, arse up across her lap.

The evening before she was scheduled to return to the facility Claire Brooks waited in her bedroom with her hands on her head and her nose pressed to the wall. She was dressed in full clobber.

As soon as she had opened her mouth Claire had known that she was heading upstairs. The family had been sitting down for a last supper together when Claire had interjected the proceedings with a typically ribald observation.

"After dinner, you will repair to your room," Ma had informed her.

"Yes Ma," groaned Claire.

Nothing more was said and over-dinner conversation continued as if nothing had happened.

Claire stared at the wall. Even though she was twenty seven years old she unequivocally accepted her mother's right to spank her. It was family tradition and one that she suspected both she and her sister would continue in the event that they got married and had children. Nonetheless, she wished her Ma wasn't quite so prolific. This would be her fourth trip over Ma's knee since returning for the furlough.

She had even traveled to Victoria's party sporting a red bottom following a disagreement with Ma.

Claire heard the familiar tread of Ma's feet as she began to mount the stairs. Her heart began to

Operation Scorched Arse

beat a little faster under her crisp white blouse and she licked her lips in nervous anticipation.

"So much for cool arse Christmas," Claire sighed to herself.

The Spice of Spanking

Ma Brooks came from the school of hard-whops. Besides the frequent hairbrush spankings she had received from Claire's grandmother she had attended the original Woody School.

At the time Woody's was considered one of the most prestigious school's in the nation, famed for its academic, sporting and artistic programs. It was also well-known for its strict discipline.

Chrissy Brooks attended Woodys in its heyday and shared her time there with such luminaries as Susan Lawton, Patty Hodge and Debs' mother, Penny Morton.

Despite the strict discipline Ma and her peers had enjoyed life at Woodys and had all graduated with exceptional qualifications.

Claire had grown up expecting to attend the school but just prior to enrolling the academy was forced to close its gates due to the increasing overhead it took to maintain the sprawling campus. The irony that a decade later she would be sentenced to spend seven years at the facility in its new capacity

Operation Scorched Arse

as the nation's most draconian Back to School unit had not escaped Claire or her mother.

Claire shrugged off her blazer and hung it back up in her wardrobe. She was dressed in a brand new crisp white blouse, her striped tie and a navy-blue gymslip with 'C' stitched in the center of the bib.

Ma Brooks sat down on a straight-backed armless chair and beckoned Claire over.

Claire stretched her long, lean feline body out across her mother's lap until she was positioned in a full drape. Her mother methodically began to rearrange her daughter's garments.

Ma believed that variety was the spice of spanking. She liked to vary her techniques from one spanking to the next. On the eve of Claire's return to the Back to School unit she selected a rhythm of spanking alternate cheeks, leaving a goodly interlude to allow them to burn in fully.

Claire Brooks was tough as nails and despite the occasional punch of her fist in the air and backward kick of her legs she gamely maintained a full drape throughout the first twelve spanks.

Claire lay panting over Ma's lap and waited for the crescendo. She knew what to expect, the question was just when and where?

Ma studied her handiwork. Claire's bum was a satisfying hue of crimson and slightly swollen. She looked over at a clock on the wall and patiently watched the second hand turn. Claire's bum was beginning to twitch in anticipation. Ma Brooks smiled to herself; she knew from personal experience that despite her show of bravado Claire would be reaching the peak of anxiety by now. She would be willing her mother to get it over with and at the same time praying to the Gods that she would be released. Timing was everything.

As the second hand completed its three hundred and sixty degree journey Ma removed her left hand from around her daughter's waist and reached over and pushed down on the back of Claire's neck. As Claire's nose was thrust towards the carpet her backside jerked upwards. Ma Brooks swung her brush.

The three zingers landed one on top of each other on the crown of the right cheek of Claire's backside in a blitz of fast spanks.

Claire squeezed her eyes tight and gritted her teeth as the pain overwhelmed her. Her right leg scissored back at the knee and she clenched her fists into tight balls.

Ma Brooks placed the hairbrush on the floor and began to rearrange Claire's clobber.

"Why don't you do fifteen minutes nose and toes," Ma told Claire, "and then after you've changed into something more comfortable come down stairs to the living room. You know how much your father likes to share a cognac with you before bed."

"Yes, Ma," groaned Claire as she pushed herself off her mothers lap.

The inmates returned in the usual fleet of limos, taxis and buses to register for the next installment of their Extreme Social Rehabilitation programs.

Claire threw her suitcase on the bed and began to unpack. Her roommate, Amanda San Pierre, wheeled her luggage into the study.
"Gosh, it sucks to be back," said Mandy. "Three weeks of cool arse suited me just fine."
"Speak for yourself," grumbled Claire and began to hang up her clobber.

www.ingramcontent.com/pod-product-compliance
Lightning Source LLC
LaVergne TN
LVHW011423080426
835512LV00005B/237